SOUNDTRACK
of the Soul

the beatitudes *of* Jesus

A Christmas Journey: Filled with Wonder, Marked by the Cross (2007)

Under the Radar: A Conversation on Spiritual Leadership (2007)

Discipline of Surrender: Biblical Images of Discipleship (2005)

La Disciplina: de la sumisión (2005)

SoulCraft: How God Shapes Us Through Relationships (2005)

A Passion for Christ: An Evangelical Christology (2002)

The Easy Yoke: Jesus' Strategy for Living (1995)

Selling Jesus: What's Wrong with Marketing the Church (1993)

Finding Spiritual Direction: The Challenges and Joys of Christian Growth (1991)

Choices of the Heart: Christian Ethics for Today (1990)

Christian Living In A Pagan Culture (1980)

SOUNDTRACK
of the Soul
the beatitudes *of* Jesus

Douglas D. Webster

CLEMENTS PUBLISHING
Toronto

This North American edition first published in 2009 by

Clements Publishing
213-6021 Yonge Street
Toronto, Ontario
M2M 3W2 Canada
www.clementspublishing.com

Book design by Pagesetters Services Pte Ltd, Singapore
www.pagesetters.com.sg

Library and Archives Canada Cataloguing in Publication

Webster, Douglas D
   Soundtrack of the soul: the beatitudes of Jesus / Douglas D. Webster.

Includes bibliographical references.
ISBN 978-1-894667-91-3

   1. Beatitudes—Meditations. 2. Beatitudes—Sermons. 3. Jesus
Christ—Teachings—Meditations. 4. Christian life. I. Title.

BT382.W434 2008   242'.5   C2008-906042-3

for

Jim and Lori Meals

Acknowledgements

The author and publisher wish to thank
Susan Montoya for her creative work on the cover,
Jim Meals for his editorial assistance, and
Jonathan Hoffner for his cover photo.

Contents

Foreword

Soundtrack of the soul is a simple metaphor for listening to Jesus. My focus is on Jesus' playlist—the beatitudes. I offer no critique here of the anthems of the age or the latest hits that you have downloaded on your iPod. The book is about Jesus and Life. My aim is to let the voice of Jesus come through and resonate in our souls. I will not assault you with my musical tastes and preferences, but I hope to communicate in a simple, straightforward manner what Jesus taught. I want you to hear Jesus on the power of soul-poverty over pride and the meaning of true joy found in genuine sorrow. Every track on Jesus' soundtrack is counter-cultural. Meekness, mercy and purity of heart may not be big hits in the world, but to those with ears to hear they are rhythms of grace. Jesus on peacemaking and persecution raises a voice of hope in a world bent on putting people down. Download the Beatitudes by Jesus and you may find your own voice—a voice of humility and hope, repentance and sorrow, confidence and peace. Living like Jesus begins with listening to Jesus.

1

Starting Over

"Blessed are the poor in spirit,
for theirs is the kingdom of heaven."

Matthew 5:3

The first three beatitudes strike at the heart of the so-called good life and attack virtually everything we know about pursuing happiness. Culture has virtually enshrined self-esteem and personal pride as the hallmark of our educational philosophy. Our prevailing mantra is believe in yourself. Counseling and therapy have taught us to blame a host of evils for our problems: bad parents, difficult circumstances, dysfunctional families, poor schools, peer pressure, etc. Ever since we were young the world's soundtrack has been on the playlist, fostering our discontent. Sinatra belted out "I Did It My Way," the Beatles asked, "Why Don't We Do It In the Road?" and Sheryl Crow smirked through her "All I Wanna Do Is Have Some Fun" life verse to the detriment of the American soul. Self-esteem and self-assertion are the dogmas of the American Dream. In three short lines, Jesus takes on the modern success ethic, the therapeutic culture and the existential quest to realize our human potential.

Jesus takes them down, one at a time, when he says,

You're blessed when you're at the end of your rope. With less of you there is more of God and his rule.

You're blessed when you feel you've lost what is most dear to you. Only then can you be embraced by the One most dear to you.

> *You're blessed when you're content with just who you are—no more, no less. That's the moment you find yourselves proud owners of everything that can't be bought.*
>
> Matthew 5:3-5, The Message

Blessed are the poor in spirit

This is a startling statement to begin with, because the great effort of human existence is to overcome poverty. Material self-sufficiency is the base line goal of every able-bodied adult. But understanding poverty in dollars and cents is not the best way to interpret the first beatitude. The Greeks had two words to describe the poor. πτωχοὶ *(ptochos)*, "which is the adjective to describe, not one who is simply poor, but one who is completely destitute" and πένης *(penes)*, which meant frugal.[1] The more emphatic word, πτωχοὶ is used to translate Jesus' Aramaic message. The same word describes "a beggar πτωχοὶ named Lazarus," whom Jesus contrasted with a rich man who was dressed in purple and fine linen and lived in luxury (Luke 16:20). πτωχοὶ is also used for the poor widow who put in two copper coins (Mark 12:42). In Jesus' parable of the Great Banquet, the word is used to describe those who are out on the highways and byways: "Go out quickly into the streets and alleys of the town and bring in the poor, the crippled, the blind and the lame" (Luke 14:21). When the apostle James warned against showing favoritism he used the more extreme word, πτωχοὶ, to describe "a poor man in shabby clothes" in contrast to a wealthy person wearing a gold ring and fine clothes (James 2:2).

Behind all these New Testament pictures is the Old Testament understanding of the poor. The poor are distinguished from the slothful, the vagrant, the thief, and the addict. The poor are oppressed because they are orphaned or widowed or victims of injustice (Job 29:12-17; Psalm 12:5; Isaiah 3:14). The Law of God protected the poor (Exodus 22:22f) and the prophets showed great sensitivity to the poor and came to their defense. Amos cried out against oppressors: "They sell the righteous for silver, and the needy for a pair of sandals. They trample on the heads of the poor as upon the dust of the ground and deny justice to the oppressed" (Amos 2:6-7). The Lord is seen as rescuing the poor "from those too strong for them, the poor and needy from those who rob them" (Psalm 35:10).

The poor includes all people who understand that they are dependent upon the Lord. That definition encompasses those who are wealthy and influential. King David cries out, "Hear, O Lord, and answer me, for I am poor and needy" (Psalm 86:1) and "This poor man called, and the Lord heard him; he saved him out of all his troubles" (Psalm 34:6). The Old Testament meaning of the poor describes those who are helpless and humble, who turn to God in prayer, acknowledge their great need and seek his help. This is the meaning that lies behind Jesus' first Beatitude. The shorter form in the Gospel of Luke, "Blessed are the poor, for yours is the kingdom of God" (Luke 6:20) should be understood in the light of this Old Testament understanding. When Matthew writes, "Blessed are the poor in spirit," he is drawing out the Hebrew meaning. He describes those "who in affliction have confidence only in God."[2] As the psalmist said, "I am in pain and distress; may your salvation, O God, protect me....The poor will see and be glad—you who seek God, may your hearts live! The Lord hears the needy and does not despise his captive people" (Psalm 69:29,32). The poor are those who are receptive to the gospel (Matthew 11:5).

The poor acknowledge their desperate need for God and their inability to merit salvation. Jesus illustrates what he means by being poor in spirit:

> Blessed is the prodigal son, who finally comes to his senses and makes the long journey home, rehearsing in his heart his painful confession, "Father I have sinned against heaven and against you. I am no longer worthy to be called your son" (Luke 15:21).

Blessed is the repentant tax collector, who humbles himself and prays, "God have mercy on me a sinner" (Luke 18:13).

Blessed is Simon Peter, who fell at the feet of Jesus and said, "Go away from me, Lord; I am a sinful man" (Luke 5:8).

Blessed is the woman caught in adultery, who is compelled to turn to Jesus as her last hope (John 8:2-11).

Blessed is Zacchaeus for allowing the power of God to convert him: "Look, Lord! Here and now I give half of my possessions to the poor, and if I have cheated anybody out of anything, I will pay back four times the amount" (Luke 19:8).

There are also plenty of illustrations in the gospels of those who were not poor in spirit.

Instead of receiving God's blessing, there was confusion in the mind of the religiously well-off Nicodemus and sadness in the heart of the self-sufficient rich young ruler. Self-righteousness blocked the grace of God in the heart of the Pharisee who looked down on the tax collector and Judas' indignation robbed him, one of Jesus very own professing disciples, from following the Savior.

The real contradiction and opposition to being poor in spirit is not wealth but pride. Spurgeon said, "The greatest unfitness for Christ is our own imaginary fitness." We have to be at the end of our resources, our merit, our power, our wisdom, and our hope, before we are open to God's mercy. This is why Eugene Peterson translates the first beatitude: *You're blessed when you're at the end of your rope. With less of you there is more of God and his rule.*

In the midst of the Watergate investigations, Chuck Colson, President Nixon's confidant and lead attorney, visited the home of Tom Phillips, President of the Raytheon corporation. These two powerful men sat in the screened-in porch on a hot, humid summer evening talking about life. Phillips explained to Colson how his success at Raytheon was not enough: "I felt a terrible emptiness. Sometimes I would get up in the middle of the night and pace the floor of my bedroom or stare out into the darkness for hours at a time....There was a big hole in my life. I began to read the Scriptures, looking for answers. Something made me realize I needed a personal relationship with God and it forced me to search. It may be hard to understand," Tom explained. "But I didn't seem to have anything that mattered. It was all on the surface. All the material things in life are meaningless if a person hasn't discovered what's underneath them."[3]

Phillips described how he came to the realization that what was missing in his life was a personal relationship with God through Jesus Christ. "I asked Christ to come into my life and I could feel his presence with me, His peace within me. I could sense His Spirit there with me." Colson was puzzled. He didn't understand the part about a personal relationship with Jesus and asking Christ to come into your life. Tom responded, "Chuck, I don't think you will understand what I'm saying about God until you are willing to face yourself honestly and squarely. This is the first step." Tom reached for a small paperback book, *Mere Christianity* by C. S. Lewis, to give to Chuck. "I suggest you take this with you and read it while you are on vacation." Tom started to hand it to him, then paused and said, "Let me read you one chapter."

> *"There is one vice of which no person in the world is free; which every one in the world loathes when he sees it in someone else; and of which hardly any people, except Christians, ever imagine that they are guilty of themselves. I have heard people admit that they are bad-tempered, or that they cannot keep their heads about girls or drink, or even that they are cowards. I do not think I have ever heard anyone who was not a Christian accuse himself of this vice...There is no fault which makes a person more unpopular, and no fault which we are more unconscious of in ourselves. And the more we have it ourselves, the more we dislike it in others."[4]*

C. S. Lewis called pride the Great Sin because "Pride leads to every other vice: it is the complete anti-God state of mind." Colson felt Lewis' words pounding straight at him, like a wave crashing down on him. Phillips read on,

"*In God you come up against something which is in every respect immeasurably superior to yourself. Unless you know God as that—and, therefore, know yourself as nothing in comparison—you do not know God at all. As long as you are proud you cannot know God. A proud person is always looking down on things and people: and, of course, as long as you are looking down, you cannot see something that is above you.*"[5]

"Suddenly I felt naked and unclean, my bravado defenses gone," Colson admitted to himself. "I was exposed, unprotected, for Lewis' words were describing me....Of course, I had not known God. *How could I?* I had been concerned with myself. I had done this and that, I had achieved, I had succeeded and I had given God none of the credit, never once thanking Him for any of His gifts to me. I had never thought of anything being 'immeasurably superior' to myself, or if I had in fleeting moments thought about the infinite power of God, I had not related Him to my life."[6]

Tom finished Lewis' chapter on pride and they talked for awhile. Tom read some passages in the Bible and then they prayed together. Colson had never prayed with anyone before, except for prayers before a meal. He was moved by Tom's prayer because it sounded as if Tom were speaking directly and personally to God, but he couldn't bring himself to pray. Alone in the car a few minutes later, after saying goodbye, he regretted the missed opportunity. As he drove out of Tom's driveway he couldn't control his tears. "What kind of weakness is this?" he angrily thought to himself. But he was crying so hard now he had to pull over to the side of the road, not more than a hundred yards from the entrance to Tom's driveway. Colson writes,

"With my face cupped in my hands, head leaning forward against the wheel, I forgot about machismo, about pretenses, about fears of being weak. And as I did, I began to experience a wonderful feeling of being released. Then came the strange sensation that water was not only running down my cheeks, but surging through my whole body as well, cleansing and cooling as it went. They weren't tears of sadness and remorse, nor of joy—but somehow, tears of relief.

And then I prayed my first real prayer. 'God, I don't know how to find You, but I'm going to try! I'm not much the way I am now, but somehow I want to give myself to You." I didn't know how to say more, so I repeated over and over the words: Take me."[7]

William Barclay summarizes the meaning of the first beatitude: "...We see it describes the person who has fully realized his own inadequacy, his own worthlessness, and his own destitution, and who has put his whole trust in God. It describes the person who has realized that by himself life is impossible but that with God all things are possible; the person who has become so dependent on God that he has become independent of everything else in the universe."

Barclay outlines three basic truths about life expressed in this first beatitude:

(1) The way to true power and wisdom lies "through the realization of helplessness." "...The way to goodness lies through the confession and the acknowledgment of sin.... If a person is ill, the first necessity is that he should admit and recognize that he is ill, and that then he should seek for a cure in the right place. The way to knowledge begins with the admission of ignorance. This first beatitude affirms the basic fact that the first necessity towards the attainment of fullness is a sense of need."[8] *We need God above all else.*

(2) The first beatitude re-evaluates the meaning of wealth.

"...true wealth can never consist in the possession of things. The person who has nothing but money...is poverty-stricken. The essential characteristic of material things is their insecurity....The person who has put his trust in that which his own skill or ingenuity can acquire has put his trust in the wrong place, and that before life ends will make the tragic discovery that he has done so."[9] *We need true wealth, the wealth that cannot be obtained through our own self-effort.*

(3) "...The way to independence lies through dependence, and the way to freedom lies through surrender.... Independence must come from complete dependence upon God. If ever a person is to know true freedom, that freedom must come through complete surrender to God."[10] *True freedom is found in God alone.*

Thus, the *meaning* of the first beatitude is consistent with the *promise* of the first beatitude. The blessing of being poor in spirit is the Kingdom of God. It is not a future place nor a utopian dream. It is here and now. It is a spiritual kingdom, but make no mistake it is a real kingdom. The Kingdom of God describes the realm in which God rules, the community of one Lord, one Faith, one baptism, and the sphere of life dominated by the sovereign Lord. The beatitudes begin and end on this promise. The Kingdom of Heaven, (which is the same as the Kingdom of God), belongs to those who are poor in spirit and to those who are persecuted because of righteousness. The beatitudes are framed by this promise and it is this promise of the Kingdom of heaven in which all the other promises, such as comfort, ownership, fulfillment, mercy, knowing God and being known by God are contained. This Kingdom consists of a radically different kind of righteousness than that of the religious types—the scribes and Pharisees (see Matthew 5:20). We have a daily, moment by moment consciousness of this kingdom, when we pray, "Our Father in heaven, hallowed be your name, your kingdom come, your will be done on earth as it is in heaven" (Matthew 6:9-10). We put first things first when we seek first "his kingdom and his righteousness" (Matthew 6:33). This is our first priority for handling everything from basic necessities to our highest aspirations. Jesus concluded the Sermon on the Mount with a warning, "Not everyone who says to me, 'Lord, Lord,' will enter the Kingdom of heaven, but only he who does the will of my Father who is in heaven" (Matthew 7:21).

The Bible teaches us that we all need to start life over. The first beatitude shows us how to do that. Jesus begins with a profound acknowledgment of our need for God. It is not the need we readily acknowledge even when we feel needy. In fact, our preoccupation with needs often deny and distract us from our one true need. Sadly, *feeling needy and being poor in spirit* are often very different. One of the worst things we can do is try to meet our deep seated need for God with material things, feel-good relationships, and hyper activity. We need to deal with life in terms other than our superficial needs. As long as we strive to meet our needs while ignoring our deepest need —our need for God, we will fail. What is needed above all else is for Jesus Christ to meet our most real need.

Two final thoughts: First, it is important to realize that we never outgrow or move beyond the first beatitude. We never graduate from being poor in spirit. We never advance beyond this spiritual profile of the follower of Jesus Christ. It is who we are, if we are committed to Christ. The beatitudes are not an ascending order of accomplishments but the full picture of the grace of Christ at work in our lives. Years after his dramatic conversion, the apostle Paul said, "Here is a trustworthy saying that deserves full acceptance: Christ Jesus came into the world to save sinners—of whom I am the worst. But for that very reason I was shown mercy so that in me, the worst of sinners, Christ Jesus might display his unlimited patience as an example for those who would believe in him and receive eternal life. Now to the King eternal, immortal, invisible, the only God, be honor and glory for ever and ever. Amen" (1 Timothy 1:15-17).

The second thought is this: the way to know Christ is to become like Jesus—the Jesus who represents himself and exemplifies the good news for life in the Sermon on the Mount. Through his actions he showed a profound affinity for those who acknowledged their dependence upon God. His ministry targeted the spiritually poor. But even more than that, in his very being he took upon himself our human condition. No one shows us what it means to be poor in spirit better than Jesus himself. "For you know the grace of our Lord Jesus Christ, that though he was rich, yet for your sakes he became poor, so that you through his poverty might become rich" (2 Corinthians 8:9). This spiritual poverty involves the elimination in us of "selfish ambition" and "vain conceit." It means cultivating the same attitude that was in Christ Jesus, who "made himself nothing, taking the very nature of a servant, being made in human likeness. And being found in appearance as a man, he humbled himself and became obedient to death—even death on a cross!" (Philippians 2:6-8).

The promise of the first beatitude parallels the blessing of Christ's humiliation. "Therefore God exalted him to the highest place and gave him the name that is above every name, that at the name of Jesus every knee should bow, in heaven and on earth and under the earth, and every tongue confess that Jesus Christ is Lord, to the glory of God the Father" (Philippians 2:9).

This then is where our life in Christ begins and remains. It begins with the need for God that only God can satisfy. The Bible describes starting over as being reborn. Nothing short of a whole new birth captures what it means to follow the Lord Jesus Christ. The imagery of new birth can be found throughout the New Testament. In order to become the children of God, we need to be born again spiritually. This new birth is not physical, biological, or sexual. The God-begotten are "not blood-begotten, not flesh-begotten, not sex-begotten" (John 1:13, The Message). In order to be a part of the kingdom of God, as Jesus made clear to Nicodemus, we need to be born again of the Spirit (John 3:3-8). Through Jesus Christ we are adopted into the family of God (Ephesians 1:5) to be transformed from the inside-out (Romans 12:2). We are saved not by doing "righteous things." We are saved by the mercy of God, "through the washing of rebirth and renewal by the Holy Spirit" (Titus 3:5). We have been given "new birth into a living hope through the resurrection of Jesus Christ from the dead" (1 Peter 1:3). We have been set free to love others deeply, from the heart, because we "have been born again, not of perishable seed, but of imperishable, through the living and enduring word of God" (1 Peter 1:23). Our sinful ways are no longer in full bloom, because "those who are born of God will not continue to sin, because God's seed remains in them" (1 John 3:9). God our Father "chose to give us birth through the word of truth, that we might be a kind of firstfruits of all he created" (James 1:18). The beatitudes are about starting over with Jesus.

2 Choosing Grief

*"Blessed are those who mourn for they
will be comforted."*

Matthew 5:4

Of all the beatitudes this is the one that seems to be the most natural for us. We need to be told to grieve, like we need to be told to breathe! Sorrow is part of life; avoiding it is like being out in a thunderstorm and trying to dodge the rain. Grief counseling is usually sought because we are grieving, not because we should be grieving. At face value being told to be sad has got to be the easiest beatitude on the list, because everyone knows how to moan and groan. Sorrow is our fate. As one of Job's counselor's said, "[We] are born to trouble as surely as sparks fly upward" (Job 5:7). Everybody knows how to cry. How does sorrow fit in to starting over?

However, the question immediately arises, what kind of grief does Jesus have in mind? "So many things to break the heart!" writes Dallas Willard, so many things to weep over: "men or women whose mates have just deserted them, leaving them paralyzed by rejection, for example; a parent in gut-wrenching grief and depression over the death of a little daughter; people in the sunset of their employable years who have lost their careers or businesses or life savings because of an 'economic downturn' or takeover of the company in which they had invested themselves."[11]

Did Jesus mean for us to associate every kind of grief and sorrow with this second beatitude? Is Jesus saying here that no matter how sad your life is, God's grace is available to you? I believe, along with Holocaust survivor Corrie ten Boom that "there is no pit so deep but God's love is not deeper still." No darkness is so thick that God's light cannot shine through and no gloom is so overwhelming that God's grace cannot overcome. Jesus said, "Come to me, all you who are weary and burdened, and I will give you rest" (Matthew 11:28). "For the Son of Man came to seek and to save what was lost" (Luke 19:10). No sorrow is beyond the scope of God's salvation, but not all sorrow and sadness invokes God's blessing. The grief we are meant to feel deeply and personally is our very own guilt, not the nastiness of the world with all of its evil and injustice. The primary concern in the second beatitude is not how the world has wronged us, but how we have wronged the world.

The real meaning of this beatitude, writes William Barclay, is: "Blessed is the person who is moved to bitter sorrow at the realization of his [or her] own sin."[12] This is the kind of mourning that is receptive, rather than resistant, to the mercy of God. It is the grief that is grateful for the grace of God. When Jesus gave the beatitudes, he may have had Isaiah 61 in mind. The parallels are striking:

> *"The Spirit of the Sovereign Lord is on me, because the Lord has anointed me to preach good news to the poor. He has sent me to bind up the brokenhearted, to proclaim freedom for captives and release for the prisoners, to proclaim the year of the Lord's favor and the day of vengeance of our God, to comfort all who mourn, and provide for those who grieve in Zion..."* Isaiah 61:1-2

To mourn in this way, is to grieve the loss of our innocence, to lament our unrighteousness and to be filled with sorrow because of our sinfulness. The tragedy of this world is not primarily social and political, it is personal. It begins with us. British author G. K. Chesterton was asked to write a magazine article on the subject, "What's wrong with the universe?" He responded to the editor's request with two words, 'I am.'

In his epistle, James referred to the kind of mourning Jesus had in mind when he exhorted believers:

> *"Come near to God and he will come near to you. Wash your hands, you sinners, and purify your hearts, you double-minded. Grieve, mourn and wail. Change your laughter to mourning and your joy to gloom. Humble yourselves before the Lord, and he will lift you up."*
>
> James 4:8-9

James' spiritual direction was intended to penetrate comfort zones and shake casual, compromising Christians from their apathy. In an age of entertainment, when nearly everyone wants to be upbeat and lighthearted, James calls for repentance. He challenges Christians to grieve, mourn and wail over their selfishness—their sinfulness.

> *"The sacrifices of God are a broken spirit; a broken and contrite heart, O God, you will not despise."*
>
> Psalm 51:17

Peace begins with repentance. The thrust of true repentance is essentially positive. We are not only commanded to draw near to God, but we are reassured that God will draw near to us. "Humble yourselves before the Lord, and he will lift you up." (James 4:10) is a glorious promise. Repentance leads to transformation. Remorse gives way to joy. This must strike most people as counter-intuitive and very paradoxical. The good news for life begins with the bad news about us. But from another angle, this makes perfect sense. How can we start over without honestly admitting that we need to start over? How can we be reborn without repentance?

The word that Jesus used for mourning was meant to convey a depth of sorrow, not a sentimental self-pity but a true brokenheartedness. The word he chose for comfort was also special. It referred to "the ultimate consolation and encouragement that God alone can effect for those whose mourning expresses the sense of total loss and helplessness. It is part of the future consummation when God will destroy sin and death and 'wipe away all tears' (Rev 21:4)."[13] Thus, the state of blessedness offered by Jesus in the beatitudes involves a distinctive kind of sorrow and a very unique promise of comfort.

Clearly, not all grief is the same and much of what we mourn over has no effect on bringing us closer to the Lord. The apostle Paul distinguished between *"godly sorrow"* and *"worldly sorrow."* He said, "Godly sorrow brings repentance that leads to salvation and leaves no regret, but worldly sorrow brings death." He then went on to elaborate on the benefits of godly sorrow: "See what this godly sorrow has produced in you: what earnestness, what eagerness to clear yourselves, what indignation, what alarm, what longing, what concern, what readiness to see justice done" (2 Corinthians 7:10-11). It is important for us to examine the kinds of grief and sorrow that prevent us from experiencing the sorrow that leads to joy and the grief that turns to gratitude.

Two life strategies that leave us incapable of expressing the kind of grief that leads us to God's grace are the pursuit of unhappiness and disappointment with God. Both of these approaches to life easily interfere with our response to the Gospel for life.

The Pursuit of Unhappiness

The title from Paul Watzlawick's book captures how many people live: *The Situation is Hopeless, But Not Serious.* He contends that many pursue *unhappiness* by investing in the wrong kind of grief. To begin with, they cultivate a seriously unserious attitude toward life. They devote themselves to trivial matters with a passion that absorbs all their energy. They insist on their own way with heroic determination. They make the past into "an inexhaustible reservoir of nostalgic misery." They blame "God, the world, fate, nature, chromosomes and hormones, society, parents, relatives, the police, teachers, doctors, bosses, and especially [their] friends" for the misery of their life. They rewrite the beatitude to read: "Blessed are those who blame others for they will feel better about themselves."

Those who pursue unhappiness tell themselves relentlessly, "Everyday in every way things are getting worse and worse." To illustrate how we are tempted to work ourselves up into a distracted state of discomfort, Watzlawick suggests the following exercise:

> "Sit quietly in a comfortable chair and concentrate on your shoes. It should not take you too long to realize, perhaps for the first time, how very uncomfortable it is to wear shoes. It does not matter how well they seemed to fit until this moment, because you will now become aware of pressure points and other unpleasant sensations, like friction, the bending of your toes, the tightness of the laces, heat or cold, and the like. Repeat the exercise until the wearing of shoes, until now a simple and trivial necessity, becomes a decidedly uncomfortable problem."[14]

If we can generate soul-distracting anxiety by just thinking about our shoes, think what we can do if we concentrate on people who annoy us and offend us. We can magnify other people's faults to such a degree that we never think about our own sin.

If you really want to be unhappy, develop a mind-set that magnifies all risk factors and learns to perpetuate problems beyond their customary duration. Imagine the worst and it will usually happen. Instead of becoming spiritually perceptive, become psychologically paranoid. Imagine that people are talking behind your back. Every whisper and every giggle is directed against you. Then cultivate the notion that you are unlovable and accuse all those who attempt to love you of some ulterior motive. Cover up your true need for God by trying to meet any and all needs of others. Assure your own disillusionment by developing a co-dependent relationship.

In other words, need to be needed by a needy person whose needs will never be met.

The pursuit of unhappiness leaves us mourning for all the wrong things. The devil would like nothing better than for us to be distracted by frustrations, pet peeves, irritations, and inconveniences, because we are then distracted from the real sorrow that is open to God's grace and mercy.

Disappointment with God

How does the second beatitude, "blessed are those who mourn," apply to the church's walking wounded? Why are there so many unhappy and disgruntled people in the church? Have we missed out on the comfort of God because we have not learned how to mourn for our sin? Should poor parents, lousy pastors and legalistic churches diminish the significance of justification by faith in Christ and redemption through his blood shed on the Cross?

In the early church, believers concentrated on their unworthiness and God's greatness, but we have turned this around. They were consumed with their relationship to God. They kept asking, "Am I living up to God's standard?" Whereas we seem to be preoccupied with ourselves. They focused on counting it a privilege to suffer for Christ, we seem to blame God when things don't go our way.

At least some unhappy believers remind me of the child who has grown up in a loving family, in a home where there never has been a question of parental love and support. The parents have provided for all of his physical needs and most of his material wants. The child is not spoiled but loved. There is a prudent measure of discipline and freedom suitable to the child's age. The child has not had to fend for himself but he has been supported in school, sports, friendships and other interests. He has been fed, clothed, educated, and related to with care. The dinner table has been a forum for the free expression of ideas, even ideas that run counter to parental perspectives. Nevertheless, in spite of a nurturing and loving environment, the child feels resentful and out-of-sorts. He is quiet and moody at the dinner table and sensitive to any word of correction from his parents. He no longer accepts their words of encouragement and feels belittled by their affirmation. No matter how loving his parents, life can only be one big disappointment as long as he translates his personal feelings of inadequacy and insecurity into resentment against those who love him.

Sad to say, this is what many of us are tempted to feel in our relationship with God. We have imposed our own failures, sins, shortcomings and struggles on our relationship with God. We have translated our false expectations and grandiose ideas into resentment against the very One who loves us and gave himself for us. We act as if the atonement, redemption and sanctification are not enough for us. The majesty of God the Father, the grace of the Lord Jesus Christ and the fellowship and wisdom of the Holy Spirit are taken for granted by juvenile Christians who want their vision of a perfect life or else the right to sit and complain against God. They want sympathy and empathy while they blame God for not catering to their needs, and somehow the idea has become popular to credit the casual, carnal Christian with the stature of Job.

Disappointment with God can become an existential convenience for people who prefer pity to repentance. It is easier to dwell on the ways we feel we have been sinned against than on the ways that we have sinned. Instead of looking for the Savior it is easier to look for a scapegoat. Instead of submitting to God's revelation it is easier to make excuses.

"Much of what is called Christian profession today,"
writes Dallas Willard, "involves no remorse or sorrow at

all over who one is or even for what one has done. There is little awareness of being lost or of a radical evil in our hearts, bodies, and souls—which we must get away from, which only God can deliver us. To manifest such awareness today would be regarded—and certainly by most Christians as well—as psychologically sick. It is common today to hear Christians talk of their 'brokenness.' But when you listen closely, you may discover that they are talking about their wounds, the things they have suffered, not about the evil that is in them.

"Few today have discovered that they have been disastrously wrong and that they cannot change or escape the consequences of it on their own. There is little sense of 'Woe is me! for I am undone; because I am a person of unclean lips, and I dwell in the midst of a people of unclean lips: for my eyes have seen the King, the Lord of hosts'" (Isaiah 6:5).

"Yet, without this realization of our utter ruin and without the genuine revisioning and redirecting of our lives, which that bitter realization naturally gives rise to, no clear path to inner transformation can be found."[15]

The pursuit of unhappiness combined with disappointment with God makes the second beatitude all the more necessary. "One might almost translate this second beatitude "Happy are the unhappy" in order to draw attention to the startling paradox it contains. What kind of sorrow can it be which brings the joy of Christ's blessing to those who feel it?"[16] It is the sorrow that takes seriously our own sinfulness. The sorrow that does not shy away from confession and contrition. The sorrow that does not make light of sin. Judging from a worldly point of view, it is ironic that the church that knows and feels deeply its own sinfulness is the church that experiences the greatest joy and understands the true meaning of God's grace. But what doesn't make sense to the world makes perfect sense to the follower of the Lord Jesus.

Grace-filled Grief

Grace-filled repentance, like grace-filled grief, gives our lives a true awareness of God's mercy and the depth of God's love. The Christian who glibly says, "I have no regrets," has not honestly wrestled with his or her sin and the distance between the Holy God and our sinful selves. True mourning for our sins is in tandem with the comfort that only God can bring into our lives.

In 1897 the British evangelical theologian P. T. Forsyth asked,

> "What should you think of the forgiven son [in the Parable of the Prodigal Son], who, as the pardoned years went on, never took his mercy seriously enough to give a thought to what he had brought on his father or God? If he never cared to go behind that free forgiveness which met him and feasted him without an unbraiding word; if he never sought to look deep into those eyes which had followed him, watched him, and spied him so far; if he was never moved by the amazing welcome to put himself in the depths of his Father's place; if he took it all with a light heart, and told the world that in forgiveness he felt nothing but gladness; if he said that was all we know and all we need to know; if the swift forgiveness of God made it easy for him to forgive himself and just forget the past; if the generous, patient father never became for him the Holy Father; if he felt it was needless and fruitless to enter into the dread depths of sin with the altar candle of the Lord, or explore the miracle of the Father's grace — what should you think of him then?"[17]

Basically, Forsyth is asking: What if we took our salvation for granted? What if the years go by and we never seek to understand more deeply what it means to be forgiven by the Holy, Righteous God? What if there is no trace of coming to our senses in any way deeper than when we were first converted? What if we were to go on "with a mere readiness of religious emotion, and a levity of religious intelligence which cares not to measure his sin by the finer standards of the Father's spirit...?"[18] What if instead of mourning for our sins and depending exclusively on the comfort of God's grace, we settled for "a natural goodness with philanthropy," "an easy optimism," "tasteful piety," "social refinement," "ethical sympathies," "aesthetic charm and a conscience more enlightened than saved." The failure to mourn for our sin and understand the immense value of our redemption leaves us as "flimsy saints...sold to the religious nothings of the hour with all their stupefying power; with no deepness of earth, no pilgrim's progress, no passion of sacred blood, no grasp of real life, no grim wrestling, no power with God, no mastery of the soul, no insight, no measure of it, no real power to retain for [ourselves], or for others to compel a belief in the soul, its reality or its Redeemer."

Once a mourner always a mourner. William Barclay draws out a significant perspective on what he calls the "strange progression" in Paul the apostle's self-reflection.[19] The older Paul became, the more he seemed inclined to express his own sinfulness and rejoice in the wonder of God's sovereign grace that he should be used by God.

When he wrote to the Galatians in A.D. 48 he referred to himself as "*Paul the apostle*" (Galatians 1:1), but when he wrote to the Corinthians seven years later he said, "*I am the least of the apostles, and not fit to be called an apostle*" (1 Corinthians 15:9). Eight years later, in A.D. 63, he compared himself to ordinary church members when he said, "*I am less than the least of all God's people*" (Ephesians 3:8). And at the end of his life, when he was awaiting death, he wrote to Timothy, his understudy, declaring,

> "Here is a trustworthy saying that deserves full acceptance: Christ Jesus came into the world to save sinners—of whom I am the worst. But for that very reason I was shown mercy so that in me, the worst of sinners, Christ Jesus might display his unlimited patience as an

example for those who would believe in him and receive
eternal life."

1 Timothy 1:15-16

It is fitting that we should conclude this beatitude with a
prayer of confession:

> *We are grateful, Lord God, for the comfort that You alone*
> *can give and for the peace that passes all understanding.*
> *But we confess that we are often indifferent to your*
> *comfort because we are focused on our disappointments.*
> *We are so weighed down by our concerns that we cannot*
> *be lifted up by your grace. Forgive us, Lord, for blaming*
> *others and feeling that You have let us down. Help us to*
> *embrace your redemptive grace and move forward in our*
> *walk with You. May Jesus Christ be praised. Amen.*

3

Understanding Power

"Blessed are the meek for they will inherit the earth."

Matthew 5:5

If the second beatitude initially impressed us as the most natural beatitude because everyone knows how to be sad, then the third beatitude will probably strike us as the most unnatural beatitude, because no one wants to be labeled meek. We said that in order to understand the second beatitude we must distinguish between godly sorrow, the sorrow that leads to repentance, and worldly sorrow, the sorrow that leads to resentment. When it comes to understanding the third beatitude we must distinguish between godly power, the power that leads to redemption, and worldly power, the power that leads to domination.

The beatitudes offer a character description of the follower of the Lord Jesus Christ. They do not prescribe the means of grace; they describe the state of grace. Like Moses in the wilderness, Jesus sets before us a blessing and a curse. There is a marked difference between being poor in spirit and being proud in spirit. Just as there is a great difference between mourning over our sin and complaining about our negative circumstances. This is true as well for the third beatitude: we either live according to the power of God's grace or we live according to worldly power.

The Meaning of Meekness

No one likes to be called meek, at least no self-respecting, self-assertive, with-it person, and especially no one who expects to be somebody. For many, meekness means weakness. It is not considered a character quality, but a personality disorder. The very idea of meekness is repulsive to many. It describes someone who feels inadequate, inferior, and helpless. It is linked with passivity and a lack of courage. It implies the inability to stand up for ourselves and the refusal to meet the challenges of life.

Some people make the mistake of confusing what the world thinks of meekness with what Jesus meant by meekness. One commentator describes the meek this way: "These are the shy ones, the intimidated, the mild, the unassertive. They step off the sidewalk to let others pass as if it were only right, and if something goes wrong around them, they automatically feel it must have something to do with them. When others step forward and speak up, they shrink back, their vocal chords perhaps moving but producing no sound. They do not assert their legitimate claims unless driven into a corner and then usually with ineffectual rage. But as the kingdom of the heavens enfolds them, the whole earth is the Father's—and theirs as they need it."[20]

Our translations reflect this discomfort with the word "meek." The New International Version uses the word "meek" only three times and "meekness" only once in the whole Bible (Psalm 37:11; Zephaniah 3:12; Matthew 5:5; 2 Corinthians 10:1). Whereas the Authorized Version (KJV) uses "meek" seventeen times and "meekness" fourteen times. In place of "meek" and "meekness" the NIV prefers to use "poor," "humble," "afflicted," "gentle," and "gentleness."

Some Christians might assume erroneously that the third beatitude approves a docile, dependent personality, that it is more pious to feel inadequate and inferior. Some falsely assume that becoming the world's doormat is the cross Christians are called to bear. But this is not what Jesus meant by the character quality of meekness.

As you might expect, the true meaning of meekness grows out of its usage in the Old Testament, where it means to be gentle, humble, lowly, considerate and gracious. The meek are open to God's leading (Psalm 25:9) and content with God's provision (Psalm 22:26). Jesus' third beatitude appears to come directly from Psalm 37. In this psalm David offers an extended commentary on meekness. Instead of picturing a shy, timid, and fearful person, David pictures the meek as unperturbed by evil people, self-controlled, confident in the Lord, and resolute in their faith and trust in God's sovereign care and justice. David's imperatives on meekness are sharp and concise and highlight true strength of character and inner discipline.

> *"Do not fret because of evil people...Trust in the Lord and do good...Delight yourself in the Lord...Commit your way to the Lord...Be still before the Lord and wait patiently for him...Refrain from anger and turn from wrath...A little while, and the wicked will be no more; though you look for them, they will not be found. But the meek will inherit the land and enjoy great peace."* Psalm 37:1-11

Meekness is an internal discipline and an intentional reliance upon God to accomplish his will and his work in *his way*. "I tell you the truth," Jesus said, "the Son can do nothing by himself; he can do only what he sees his Father doing, because whatever the Father does the Son also does...By myself I can do nothing" (John 5:19, 30). Meekness is a "conscious suppression of willfulness and a purposeful cultivation of willingness."[21] According to Augustine, one of the early church leaders, the only thing that matters to the meek is pleasing God: "The meek are they, to whom all their good deeds, in all the things they do well, nothing is pleasing but God; to whom in all the evils they suffer, God is not displeasing."[22]

Meekness is the openness to see God in the big picture of life and to recognize "that in all things God works for the good of those who love him, who have been called according to his purpose" (Romans 8:28). Meekness leads us to say with Paul, "I can do all things through Christ who strengthens me," and mean it not as a boast but as a confidence. Think of meekness as bold humility or aggressive patience. It is the spiritual discipline that overcomes the world. To be meek in the biblical sense is to be neither mousy nor militant. It strikes the mean between being passive and pushy, cowardly and reckless, lenient and harsh. Meekness is a one word summary of greatness, but not as the world defines greatness.

Jesus confirmed the meaning of meekness when he said, "Come to me, all you who are weary and burdened, and I will give you rest. Take my yoke upon you and learn from me, for I am meek (or gentle) and humble in heart, and you will find rest for your souls. For my yoke is easy and my burden is light" (Matthew 11:28-30).

The Will to Power

The third beatitude concentrates on the difference between relying on God's power and striving to obtain and maintain our own power. One path leads to submission and service, the other leads to superiority and privilege. God's power inspires obedience, faith and trust; worldly power triggers ambition, pride, and self-reliance. Worldly power is based on the law of the jungle; God's power is centered around the throne of the slain Lamb, who is worthy to receive glory and honor and power. Worldly power is captured in Darwin's thesis, "the survival of the fittest," and in Machiavelli's conviction that the end justifies the means. Nietzsche contended that the essence of humanity without God is the will to power. In contrast, the meaning of godly power is captured in Paul's saying, "I can do all things through Christ who gives me strength" (Philippians 4:13) and in God's word, "My grace is sufficient for you, for my power is made perfect in weakness" (2 Corinthians 12:8).

According to Jesus, everything we've ever been told about getting ahead in the world is wrong. The world says, "Believe in yourself." Jesus says, "Believe in me." The world says, "Strive to be number one." Jesus says, "The last shall be first, and the first shall be last." The world says, "Winning isn't everything, it's the only thing." Jesus says, "He who finds his life will lose it, and he who loses his life for my sake will find it." The world says, "Don't get mad, get even." Jesus says, "Love your enemy and pray for those who persecute you." The world teaches, "Stand up for your rights." Jesus teaches, "Lay down your life." The world teaches us to assert ourselves; Jesus teaches us to deny ourselves. The world says the one with the most toys wins; Jesus says, "You can gain the whole world and lose your soul."

Meekness describes the person who has nothing to prove, no one to impress, no power to acquire and no glory to seek after. The meek do not force their will on others, nor change their will to win the favor of others. The meek can afford to embrace love, humility, gentleness and patience, and reject manipulation, coercion, and deception, because their hearts are at rest and their destiny is secure. There are numerous biblical examples of people who were free to rest in the sovereign will of God. They were not consumed by the will to power, but instead were committed to the power of God. Abel, Abraham, Moses and David, to name a few, illustrate the meaning of meekness and the power of God. Yet, even they illustrate the seductive nature of the will to power. But the greatest example of meekness is revealed in the triune God, Father, Son, and Holy Spirit.

The Meekness of God

In the biblical sense of the word, Jesus was the picture of meekness. This led the apostle Paul to base his ministry on "the meekness and gentleness of Christ" (2 Corinthians 10:1). Paul exhorted the followers of Christ to "do nothing out of selfish ambition or vain conceit" because Christ "did not consider equality with God something to be grasped, but made himself nothing, taking the very nature of a servant, being made in human likeness. And being found in appearance as a man, he humbled himself and became obedient to death—even death on the cross!" (Philippians 2:3-8). The meekness inherent in Jesus' incarnation and earthly ministry climaxes in his sacrifice on the cross, but the meekness of God is not limited to the second member of the Trinity. As we might have expected, meekness and majesty are perfectly consistent throughout the Godhead.

Meekness is a fitting description of the living God who reveals himself slowly, personally, and with great reserve. The "hidden God", as Luther liked to say, is the God who "works righteousness and justice for all the oppressed"; who "made known his ways to Moses, and his deeds to the people of Israel: The Lord who is compassionate and gracious, slow to anger, abounding in love" (Psalm 103:6-8). The history of redemption is a reflection of God's meekness. The God of all creation walked with Adam and Eve in the garden and the Lord of the Nations choose to work through Abraham and his descendants to bring about salvation. He called Moses out of the wilderness with a burning bush and revealed his personal name, *I Am*. He anointed David, a man after his own heart, as his representative and he appointed the prophets to declare his word. The climax of God's great salvation history story is reached in the Incarnation at the point of God's greatest humility and vulnerability, but the victory of God's redemptive love is never in doubt. Inherent in this entire history is the meekness of God that seeks to love and forgive us. All God's grace-filled effort is to the end that we might be healed and restored. The divine rationale is no secret: "'Not by might nor by power, but by my Spirit,' says the Lord Almighty" (Zechariah 4:6). The fact that God should work this way is beyond the rationale of fallen human kind and the history of dynasties, dictators, wars and empires.

The meekness of God is made especially evident in Jesus' reticence to claim the title of Messiah and in his reserve in explaining the work of the Cross. Why was Jesus reluctant to say boldly, "I am the Messiah!"? Actually, Jesus' elusive response fits a pattern in which he avoided direct answers to questions about his authority. He was reluctant to publicize his work. When the Jewish religious leaders confronted him, demanding to know by what authority he taught and acted, he declined to comment (Luke 20:1-8). He repeatedly demanded secrecy from those he healed (Mark 1:44; 5:43; 7:36; 8:26), and he insisted on silence when the demon-possessed cried out that Jesus was the Son of God (Mark 1:34; Luke 4:41). Even the disciples were warned not tell anyone that he was the Christ (Matthew 16:20) or to reveal their experience of Jesus' Transfiguration (Matthew 17:9).

True messianic consciousness is disclosed by Jesus precisely in his endeavor to disassociate himself from popular appeal and power politics. Both the masses and the opposition responded to Jesus in nationalistic fervor, seeing him either as a new hero for a popular uprising or a fresh threat to the status quo. Jesus sought to redefine his messiahship according to biblical revelation. For Jesus to have allowed his role to be defined by contemporary messianic expectation would have been tantamount to yielding to the initial temptations in the wilderness. Jesus subjected himself and his followers to the painful course of messianic redefinition in terms anticipated in the Old Testament.

Not until the end did Jesus clearly and publicly admit he was the Messiah. When the high priest asked, "Are you the

Christ, the Son of the Blessed One?" Jesus responded directly, "I am...And you will see the Son of Man sitting at the right hand of the Mighty One and coming in the clouds of heaven" (Mark 14:61-62). The perceptive German theologian Helmut Thielicke observed,

> *"It is striking that Jesus uses these predicates of majesty when he is being delivered up to death, exposed to humiliation, and plunged into the passion, so that the confession of his messiahship can no longer give a wrong impression of loftiness nor lead to a theology of glory, but engulfs us in the depths of this destiny."*[23]

Perhaps there is another dimension that needs to be considered. Jesus freely uses the title of Christ only after the Resurrection, when he can point to the finished work of the Cross and the completion of the Father's will (Luke 24:26, 46). Before he claimed the title for himself, he accomplished all that the Father prepared for him to do. Only then did he employ the title Messiah instead of his familiar self-designation as the Son of Man.

Throughout his humiliation and exaltation Jesus was shown to be what he knew he was, the eternal Son of God. He was "acknowledged Messiah in fact not just *after* his passion and resurrection but *because* of his passion and resurrection—and, it must be insisted, in continuity with his own self-consciousness during the ministry" (see Acts 2:36; Romans 1:4; Hebrews 5:8-10).[24] Jesus did not clamor for a title which implied a redemptive accomplishment yet to be fulfilled through the Cross and the Resurrection. Nevertheless, he consistently disclosed that the kingdom of God had come through his own person and work. God's meekness was on display in Jesus' reticence to claim the title Messiah. He did not lay claim to the title until it was obvious that His death on the Cross proved that political power was not the means to finish what the Father sent him to accomplish.

The meekness of God is also evident in the reserve with which the Gospels explain the Atonement. Publicity would have been completely inconsistent with the preparations that had been made for the Atonement throughout salvation history by means of illustrations, types, and the sacrificial system. God in his meekness has always allowed his actions to speak louder than his words. He did not give Cain and Abel a theology lesson before choosing Abel's sacrifice and disqualifying Cain's. He did not carefully explain to Abraham how the command to sacrifice his son Isaac was a picture of the will of the Father in giving up his one and only Son. Nor did God explain to Job that he would take a world of unjust suffering and nail it to the cross. He let King David and the prophets discover that a broken and contrite heart meant more than sacrifices.

It would be foolish to conclude from the lack of publicity and pedantic instruction about the Cross in the Gospels that the meaning of the Cross is somehow disqualified for lack of information and doctrinal explanation. Later, the Epistles will explain and expound on the wonder of the Atonement, but it is helpful to contemplate the reasons for this initial reserve. First of all, there is more going on within the relationships of the triune God than we could begin to imagine, much less figure out and reduce to bullet points. P. T. Forsyth wisely observes:

> "Christ came not to say something, but to do something. His revelation was more action than instruction. He revealed by redeeming. The thing He did was not simply to make us aware of God's disposition in an impressive way. It was not to declare forgiveness. It was certainly not to explain forgiveness. And it was not even to bestow forgiveness. It was to effect forgiveness, to set up the relation of forgiveness both in God and man. ...The great mass of Christ's work was like a stable iceberg. It was hidden. It was His dealing with God, not man. The great thing was done with God. It was independent of our knowledge of it. The greatest thing ever done in the world was done out of sight. The most ever done for us was done

behind our backs. Only it was we who had turned our backs. Doing this for us was the first condition of doing anything with us."[25]

Secondly, the meekness of God produces a method of relating that good parents can appreciate. It is not the habit of thoughtful, loving parents to document and elaborate on everything they do for their children. It is enough for parents that their children know of their love and benefit from their nurture and care. In time, children grow up and mature and begin to realize how much their parents have done for them. Worldly power is always striving for recognition, promising more than it can deliver, and advancing its own agenda, but that is not how our heavenly Father works. P. T. Forsyth offers an important perspective:

"It would not be like the grace of God, it would be ungracious, if He came forgiving man and yet laying more stress on what it cost Him to do it than His joy, fullness, and freedom in doing it. You find poor human creatures who never can overlook your mistake without conveying to you that it is as much as they can do. They think no little of themselves for doing it. They take care that you shall never forget their magnanimity in doing it. They keep the cost of your forgiveness ever before you. And the result is that it is not forgiveness at all. How miserable a thing it is instead! How this spirit takes the charm from the reconciliation! How it destroys the grace of it! How penurious the heart it betrays! How it shrivels the magnanimity it parades! How grudging, how ungodlike it is! How unfatherly! What an ungracious way of dealing with the graceless!"

"That is not God's way of forgiveness. His Fatherhood has the grand manner. It has not only distinction, but delicacy. He leaves us to find out in great measure what it cost—slowly, with the quickened heart of the forgiven, to find that out. Christ never told His disciples He was Messiah till it was borne in on them by contact with Him. He never told them till, by the working of the actual

Messiahship upon them, they found it out. Revelation
came home to them as discovery. It burst from experience.
So gracious is God with His revelation that He actually
lets it come home to us as if we had discovered it. That is
His fine manner — so to give as if we had found."[26]

The meekness of God is revealed in God the Father's reserve, and in God the Son's reticence, and in God the Spirit's selflessness. Divine meekness has no parallel in the history of man-made gods and in the religions of human origin and invention. And it is essential that we realize that this meekness is not for show, but is inherent in the will of God and in the internal communion of the Father, Son and Holy Spirit. It is the meekness of the Father that wills to redeem humankind through love and grace. It is the meekness of the Son that proves the Father's will and preserves the integrity of the Incarnation. And it is the meekness of the Spirit who was sent not to speak on his own behalf, but to bear witness to Jesus Christ (John 16:13-15). If the triune God chose to reveal, redeem and sanctify us in this way, we ought to embrace meekness as the way of life most consistent with following Christ.

The Promise of Meekness

The strength to be meek lies in the promises of God. "Blessed are the meek, for they will inherit the earth." The reason we can afford to be meek is because of the grace of God in the present and because of the promise of God for the future. It is worth noting that Jesus enlarged the promise expressed in Psalm 37:11 and expanded its meaning. The psalmist envisioned the Promised Land, but Jesus promised the whole earth. The reason we can be meek is because "we are more than conquerors through Him who loved us" (Romans 8:37). We fight not for victory but from victory and the "the weapons we fight with are the not weapons of the world" (2 Corinthians 10:4). Jesus said it clearly, "In this world you will have trouble. But take heart! I have overcome the world" (John 16:33).

The benefits of meekness are both immediate and everlasting. The third beatitude is a constant reminder to choose God's power over worldly power. Jesus-style meekness makes the yoke of Christ easy and saves us from the burden of worried productivity and wrong-headed activism. It frees Christians from the pressure of a spiritual full-court press designed to prove that we are worthy of God's approval and people's affirmation. Meekness cuts through the sloth and busywork of religious activities and teaches us to rely on Christ rather than our own efforts. Negatively, meekness removes the pressure tactics, manipulation and marketing techniques from our evangelism and church growth; positively, meekness gives us a love for people and an ability to approach people with a genuine concern for their welfare and their relationship to God. Meekness refuses to fret because of evildoers and rejects any militancy that would force people to follow God against their will. Meekness heals and strengthens our easily bruised egos and over-sensitive spirits by refocusing our lives on Christ.

It is helpful to be around people who are meek, because they tend to make us better Christians than we want to be. The most powerful people in the Kingdom of God are not those who exude self-confidence and success, nor are they the busybodies who lay a guilt-trip on others, nor are they the excitable saints who show off their emotions for all to see.

When my wife's parents Paul and Merry Long served among the Baluba people of the Kasai in Congo back in 1954, they met Tshiela Harieta, a graceful old African woman. Tshiela had been the third wife of an important tribesman across the river. When her husband died she was faced with two choices: she could either become a prostitute or a shaman. Since she had become a follower of Jesus Christ shortly before her husband died she refused both options and fled across the river to become a member of the New Tribe. Tshiela worked at the mission hospital caring for the patients who had no family members to help them or to cook meals for them. Often she would show up at the screen door of the Long's home in search of food for needy patients. Paul was not always pleased to see Tshiela because it usually meant giving up something that was in short supply, such as meat, to feed a total stranger. One morning Tshiela arrived in their yard with an old naked woman, who was not a Christian and from another tribe. Annoyed, Paul declined Tshiela's request to help clothe the woman on grounds that he would be showing partiality. Since he couldn't help them all, he should not help just one. Undeterred, Tshiela left, only to return a short time later. She gave her characteristic greeting, and when Paul came to the door, he found Tshiela outside on the back porch squatting— naked like the old woman who had come in the morning. Paul asked her why she was naked and she explained that she had given her clothes to the old woman. "Then I guess you will sleep cold tonight, Tshiela," Paul said with firmness.

"Oh no, Muambi," Tshiela replied. "I gave my dress away because you could not show partiality to the pagan woman with all the others around us in need, and that is right. But I am of the New Tribe of the Jesus People and you could not leave me in need, could you?"

A little while later Tshiela padded down the path toward the hospital wearing a new dress and a new blanket draped around her shoulders. She thanked Paul with a happy laugh and departed singing her funny little song about the goodness of God. Paul remembers the meekness of Tshiela and her ability to help him be a better Christian than he would have been without her.[27]

Only the meek can say with the apostle, "I am not ashamed of the gospel, because it is the power of God for the salvation of everyone who believes" (Romans 1:16). The meek find in the message of the cross the power and wisdom of God. Instead of a spirit of timidity and weakness or a spirit of pride and coercion, they have been given the Spirit of power, of love and of self-discipline (2 Timothy 1:7). Whenever we defend or promote the gospel of Christ by means of worldly power we discredit our crucified Lord. The only way to commend the gospel is the Jesus way.

4

Feeding the Soul

*"Blessed are those who hunger and thirst
for righteousness, for they will be filled."*

Matthew 5:6

Jesus presented the beatitudes as a complete portrait of the committed disciple. Each beatitude depends upon and in a sense contains all the other beatitudes. To be meek in the biblical sense of the word is to be poor in spirit; to mourn for our sin is to show mercy. The beatitudes are like the colors in a rainbow. They are derived from a single source of light—the Light of Christ, refracted into an array of distinguishable yet inseparable colors. The more we reflect on the beatitudes the more we realize that the order in which Jesus gave them matters. Each beatitude seems to build upon the previous beatitude. There is a logical progression from acknowledging our dependence upon God to mourning for our sin. Biblical meekness follows naturally from godly repentance and produces a hunger and thirst for righteousness. The beatitudes redefine the self from the inside out. Jesus begins the beatitudes with the individual's personal awareness of God ("Blessed are the poor in spirit....") and ends with the public persecuted self ("Blessed are those who are persecuted because of righteousness..."). Each beatitude is best understood in the light of all the other beatitudes.

This perspective is important because by the time we reach the fourth beatitude we have come to some understanding of righteousness. Any notion of self-righteousness has been ruled out by the first three beatitudes. The righteousness we are challenged to hunger and thirst for is not a righteousness that feeds our pride, boosts our ego, or leads us to think that we are better than other people. It is the righteousness of God, the righteousness that puts us in right relationship with God and in right relationship with his sovereign moral order. It is the righteousness that is *by* God, *for* God and *of* God. It is, in fact, the righteousness of Jesus.

The Meaning of Righteousness

We cannot separate the meaning of righteousness from the Author of the beatitudes because it is his righteousness that makes us righteous. Moreover he defines the nature and scope of righteousness and empowers our righteousness. Without Jesus we have no righteousness to hunger and thirst after, because the "righteousness from God comes through faith in Jesus Christ to all who believe" (Romans 3:22). He "has become for us wisdom from God—that is, our righteousness, holiness and redemption" (1 Corinthians 1:30). He embodies in his person the meaning of righteousness. He was "tempted in every way, just as we are—yet was without sin" (Hebrews 4:15) and "God made him who had no sin to be sin for us, so that in him we might become the righteousness of God" (2 Corinthians 5:21). "He himself bore our sins in his body on the tree, so that we might die to sins and live for righteousness: by his wounds [we] have been healed" (1 Peter 2:24). It is the risen Christ who "guides [us] in paths of righteousness for his name's sake" (Psalm 23:3).

As we look ahead in the Sermon on the Mount there are four references to righteousness that shape our understanding of the meaning of righteousness in the fourth beatitude.

First, the eighth beatitude teaches us that the righteousness of God is incompatible with what the world thinks is right. "Blessed are those who are persecuted because of righteousness, for theirs is the kingdom of heaven" (Matthew 5:10).

Second, Jesus warns us that this righteousness is different

from the righteousness associated with external religious practice—no matter how sincere. "For I tell you that unless your righteousness surpasses that of the Pharisees and the teachers of the law, you will certainly not enter the kingdom of heaven" (Matthew 5:20).

Third, this righteousness does not call attention to ourselves and to our acts of piety. "Be careful not to do your 'acts of righteousness' before people, to be seen by them. If you do, you will have no reward from your Father in heaven" (Matthew 6:1).

Fourth, this righteousness is more important than anything else in life. To pursue righteousness becomes the believer's main ambition and goal in life. Jesus challenged his disciples to put first things first. "But seek first his kingdom and his righteousness, and all these things will be given to you as well. Therefore do not worry about tomorrow, for tomorrow will worry about itself. Each day has enough trouble of its own" (Matthew 6:34).

Jesus understood this heart righteousness to be counter-cultural, non-religious, non-legalistic and selfless. Such righteousness should not be confused with "a natural goodness with philanthropy," "an easy optimism," "tasteful piety," "social refinement," "ethical sympathies," "aesthetic charm and a conscience more enlightened than saved."[28]

The disciples discovered that Jesus came to establish the Law, not undermine it; to complete it, not condemn it. By reducing it to an external religious authority and legal code, the Pharisees short-circuited the intended meaning of the Law. They were guilty of missing the meaning of the Law by substituting external religious conformity for heart righteousness. In Jesus we find the key to interpreting the Law and the Prophets. Without Him we cannot get a true perspective on righteousness. He alone restored to biblical interpretation its original and intended purpose, and set the Law in an entirely new theological context. He both established and transcended the meaning that had been lost by both the popular and the more rigorous biblical interpreters of his day.

Jesus taught that true righteousness was not imposed by a contractual obligation, but inspired by a covenant relationship. Obedience was not meant to be a duty as much as a privilege. The follower of Jesus is committed to a person, not to an idea or an ideology. The gospel of grace frees us to fulfill the Law through the righteousness of Christ and the example of Jesus. We are free from the law of sin and death. Therefore, by God's grace, we are free for faithfulness and obedience.

Come to the Sermon on the Mount "with the legalistic mind, and it is impossible and absurd; come to it with the mind of the lover, and nothing else is possible." Missionary statesman E. Stanley Jones expressed it well when he wrote, "The lover's attitude is not one of duty, but one of privilege. Here is the key to the Sermon on the Mount. We mistake it entirely if we look on it as the chart of the Christian's duty; rather it is the charter of the Christian's liberty."[29]

Boston College professor of philosophy Peter Kreeft observes, "Nowhere in the Bible do we find the humanist's prescription of 'try a little harder.' Man's answer is 'try', God's is 'trust'. Faith alone opens the door of the soul to the divine Lover who impregnates it with his own life. The Sermon on the Mount describes that life, the fruits of faith. Humanism tries to grow the fruit without the root."[30]

Jesus made it clear that righteousness is not a matter of personal opinion. Goodness is not defined by personal preference and taste. Jesus defined righteousness in a specific, definite way. We are not left to our imagination or invention, but to his revelation. In many ways the rest of the Sermon on the Mount works out personally and socially what righteousness really means in the real world. *Visible righteousness* is love instead of hate, purity instead of lust, fidelity instead of infidelity, honesty instead of dishonesty, and reconciliation instead of retaliation (Matthew 5:21-48). *Hidden righteousness* is compassion for the needy, genuine prayer and true fasting (Matthew 6:1-18). Heart righteousness is composed of Kingdom values and undivided loyalty to Christ (Matthew 6:19-24); the righteousness that is unburdened by worry, judgmental attitudes, and forced evangelism (Matthew 6:25-7:6). True righteousness chooses the way that leads to life, listens to the teachers that bear good fruit, and prefers actions to empty words (Matthew 7:13-23). This is the enduring righteousness that builds on the bedrock reality of Jesus Christ and his word (Matthew 7:24-27).

The Sermon on the Mount equates the meaning of righteousness with the fullness of the will of God. "Righteousness" is not a stodgy, stuffy religious word, but a comprehensive, powerful word that embraces justification by faith in Christ, personal holiness, the work of sanctification, and the pursuit of social justice in every sphere of life. "It would be a mistake to suppose," writes John Stott, "that the biblical word 'righteousness' means only a right relationship with God on the one hand and a moral righteousness of character and conduct on the other. For biblical righteousness is more than a private and personal affair; it includes social righteousness as well. And social righteousness, as we learn from the law and the prophets, is concerned with seeking man's liberation from oppression, together with the promotion of civil rights, justice in the law courts, integrity in business dealings and honor in home and family affairs. Thus Christians are committed to hunger for righteousness in the whole human community as something pleasing to God."[31]

The righteousness that we have by faith in Christ (Romans 1:17) leads us to offer our bodies "as instruments of righteousness" (Romans 6:13). Paul used emotionally charged language to emphasize our relationship to righteousness. We used to be slaves of sin, he reasoned, and thus "free from the control of righteousness," but since we have been set free from sin by the gift of God in Christ Jesus our Lord we are slaves of righteousness (Romans 6:19-22). When the apostle Paul used this graphic, social analogy to capture the believer's commitment to righteousness he was building on a tradition used by the Lord Jesus.

The fourth beatitude compares our longing for righteousness to being hungry and thirsty. Jesus linked our physical appetite for food and water to our desire for righteousness. Righteousness is to life what food is to the body. For the follower of Jesus Christ it is a basic necessity that we cannot live without.

Hunger and Thirst

The roots of this powerful analogy run deep in biblical thought. We are constantly reminded of the close relationship between the body and the soul. There is a physical side to being spiritual and a spiritual side to being physical. Manna in the wilderness proved that both the body and the soul have appetites that need to be satisfied. It became clear that from God's perspective there was more to life than being well fed and physically satisfied. It didn't take long for the Israelites to compare their existence in the wilderness to their fond, but distorted, remembrance of life back in Egypt. "If only we had died by the Lord's hand in Egypt! There we sat around pots of meat and ate all the food we wanted, but you have brought us out into this desert to starve this entire assembly to death" (Exodus 16:3).

Immediate material gratification is a strong temptation. By reducing life to appearances and appetites there is no vision for anything other than that which is literal, physical, and material. Our dog, Maggie, lives this kind of one-dimensional life. She's fed twice a day, morning and evening. *Science Diet Dog Food* plus a little exercise and affection make for a happy dog. We humans are in danger of copying a dog's existence, when we say to ourselves, "You have plenty of good things laid up for many years. Take life easy; eat, drink and be merry" (Luke 12:19).

Satisfying our physical appetites at the expense of our soul is a major issue in the Bible. It is fine to care about our physical well-being, but we must care first and foremost about our relationship with the Lord. We need to eat and exercise, but there is more to living than following our physical and material appetites. This was the issue that confronted Jesus in the wilderness. After fasting forty days and nights, he was hungry. The tempter came to him and said, "If you are the Son of God, tell these stones to become bread." Jesus answered, "It is written: 'Man does not live on bread alone, but on every word that comes from the mouth of God'" (Matthew 4:2-4). Jesus pointed back to the meaning of manna. He emphasized the priority of life in the Spirit over physical life alone.

To the Israelites, their Egyptian oppressors epitomized the good life. They had forgotten why God called Moses to deliver them: "I have indeed seen the misery of my people in Egypt. I have heard their crying...I am concerned about their suffering so I have come down to rescue them" (Exodus 3:7-8). They envied their oppressors and the very lifestyle that made them poor. In the wilderness all they could remember was the all you could eat Egyptian buffet. Looking back at their old way of life they seem to have forgotten the slavery and the misery. Often we are tempted to live only on the surface. When life is shrunk down to the tangible, visceral, physical and material world it seems a whole lot easier to cope than the journey of faith in a real-world wilderness. The pursuit of immediate physical pleasure is much easier than the pursuit of justice, but is it enough? Does it truly satisfy? Many seem content with a simple life-formula of convenience, comfort and entertainment. Do we have it so good physically and materially that we are too self-satisfied to hunger and thirst for anything more?

The reason God allowed Israel to experience hunger in the wilderness was so Israel would learn to turn to God. But instead of praying to God for his provision they murmured and complained and wished they were back in their old lifestyle. God responded to their need, in spite of their grumbling. They called it manna, God called it bread from heaven.

From the start manna's purpose went beyond physical nourishment. God's physical provision was meant to be a reminder of their spiritual dependence. God put the Israelites on a healthy spiritual and physical diet. The Lord had no desire to compete with Egyptian cuisine. He fed them, he didn't spoil them. What a good diet can do for our bodies, manna did for the sojourners in the wilderness.

Performance athletes are experts in nutrition. They find the right balance of carbohydrates, fat, and protein to strengthen their bodies and to keep them well-fueled. They know the science of a good diet. They know how carbohydrates help regulate fat and protein metabolism and how the body converts carbohydrates into glucose to meet energy demands and stores the excess in the muscles and liver as glycogen. They avoid fast foods and processed foods. They are sensitive to what they eat, when they eat, and how their food is prepared in order to maximize the energy impact. Tour de France riders require 7,000 calories a day to stay in shape and even then they lose weight and muscle mass. The athlete's passion to eat for health and high energy performance helps restore the power of Jesus' analogy for those who look upon eating as a social pastime and food as a simple matter of taste. Nutritious conscious, energy burning athletes bring a fresh meaning to the believer's hunger and thirst for righteousness.

The fourth beatitude challenges our appetite for God and his righteousness. Do we hunger and thirst after the wholeness of God's righteousness or are we consumed by our physical, material, and sexual appetites? Do we have a passion for righteousness and justice? The great fourth century preacher John Chrysostom, observed that hunger and thirst for food and possessions was the hallmark of covetousness. He saw Jesus challenging his followers "to transfer this desire to a new object, freedom from covetousness."[32] Chrysostom was right. If we are so absorbed with physical pleasure, material possessions, and sensual stimulation, we will never have the capacity and desire to seek first Christ's kingdom and his righteousness.

It is especially important to note that religion itself can destroy our appetite for righteousness. The apostle Paul used the strongest language to expose "enemies of the cross of Christ" whose "god is their stomach, and their glory is in their shame" (Philippians 3:18-19). Our first thought may be that Paul is referring to outright hedonists, but instead he is describing religious people who scrupulously followed ritual food laws and ignored the grace of the Lord Jesus Christ.[33] As far as Paul was concerned to covet ritualistic purity at the expense of the Cross was just as bad as being guilty of the basest bodily sins. This is why Paul emphasized to the believers at Rome that "the kingdom of God is not a matter of eating and drinking, but of righteousness, peace and joy in the Holy Spirit" (Romans 14:17).

Another way to look at this is to see how the fourth beatitude challenges the sin of sloth. Peter Kreeft calls sloth the distinctly modern sin, because it robs us of our appetite for God. We are not necessarily lazy, in fact we might be quite busy, but we are bored with God and the work of God. And to be bored with God is to be bored with everything else. We are tempted to fill up our lives with distractions and "a thousand busynesses."[34] Our capacity "to act justly and to love mercy and to walk humbly with [our] God" atrophies without exercise.

Sloth is not just laziness, it is the sinful refusal to do the work that God calls us to do. Sloth complacently ignores the fact that "the God-shaped vacuum in us is infinite and cannot be filled with any finite objects or actions."[35]

"Sloth is a cold sin, not a hot one," observes Peter Kreeft. It dismisses the work of righteousness with a shrug. "Sloth is a sin of omission, not commission."[36] "It is the sin that unobtrusively avoids Creator-attentiveness and creature-awareness, and then nosily and busily diverts attention from the great avoidance with a smoke screen of activity." Eugene Peterson continues, "Sloth is doing nothing of what we were created to do as beings made in the image of God and saved by the Cross of Christ. Sloth is laziness at the center, while the periphery is adazzle with a torrent of activity and talk."[37]

The fourth beatitude challenges the twin sins of covetousness and complacency, avarice and apathy, and warns us that if we have no appetite for righteousness we'll starve to death. C. S. Lewis describes how the fourth beatitude reveals the secret of a happy life:

> *When we want to be something other than the thing God wants us to be, we must be wanting what, in fact, will not make us happy. Those Divine demands which sound to our natural ears most like those of a despot and least like those of a lover, in fact marshall us where we should want to go if we knew what we wanted. He demands our worship, our obedience, our prostration....Yet the call is not only to prostration and awe; it is to a reflection of the Divine life, a creaturely participation in the Divine attributes which is far beyond our present desires. We are bidden to 'put on Christ,' to become like God.... God gives what He has, not what He has not: He gives the happiness that there is, not the happiness that is not. To be God — to be like God and to share His goodness in creaturely response — to be miserable — these are the only three alternatives. If we will not learn to eat the only food that the universe grows — the only food that any possible universe ever can grow — then we must starve eternally.*[38]

Fulfillment

An older generation raised on the Rolling Stones' signature song, *I Can't Get No Satisfaction*, and U2's *I Still Can't Find What I'm Looking For* ought to take notice of Jesus' radical promise of fulfillment: "Blessed are those who hunger and thirst after righteousness for they will be filled." Justification and justice come together in the one who declared:

> *"I am the bread of life. He who comes to me will never go hungry, and he who believes in me will never be thirsty... For I have come down from heaven not to do my will but to do the will of him who sent me...For my Father's will is that everyone who looks to the Son and believes in him shall have eternal life, and I will raise him up at the last day."* John 6:35-40

We are like the woman at the well. We have a hunger that cannot be satisfied by food and a thirst that cannot be quenched by water. And what Jesus said to her he says to us, "If you knew the gift of God and who it is that asks you for a drink, you would have asked him and he would have given you living water" (John 4:10).

Our thirst for life cannot be met in any other way than through Christ. Jesus made this clear when he said, "I tell you the truth, unless you eat the flesh of the Son of Man and drink his blood, you have no life in you. Whoever eats my flesh and drinks my blood has eternal life, and I will raise him up at the last day. For my flesh is real food and my blood is real drink. Whoever eats my flesh and drinks my blood remains in me, and I in him" (John 6:53-57). There are so many ways that we seek to quench the thirst for life, but there is only one way to satisfy the thirst for life.

Jesus' simple words from the cross, "I thirst," offers more commentary on the meaning of the cross than we might have imagined. It emphasizes the physical condition of suffering humanity and the purpose of God's redemptive plan. It also reminds all who are serious about following Jesus, that discipleship can be physically demanding. The fifth word of the Cross, "I thirst," underscores the physical cost of following Jesus. Can anyone look at the cross of Jesus and claim that physical health and material prosperity are a right for those who follow Jesus? Do we honestly expect to take up our cross and follow Jesus and never be worn out? Those who are committed to following Jesus will experience the demands of obedience on their emotional and physical well-being. When Jesus said, "I thirst," he reminded us that cross-bearing is not stress-free living. We were meant to share his thirst for righteousness.

But the question arises: How willing are we to let the Lord guide us along paths of righteousness, even if the way is difficult? What if the journey for God-honoring justice and righteousness is more demanding that we thought? Will we be left high and dry?

On a recent last long-distance hike in the Sierras, a friend of mine, Jim Metts, along with his son-in-law Darrin Wilson, covered a twenty-mile stretch where there was no water. They "cameled up," as Jim says with as much water as they could sensibly carry and set out for the nine-hour hike. He was somewhat nervous about the water situation, because they were dependent upon a person whom they didn't know, leaving water at their destination. If the water wasn't there, they would have had to walk another couple of hours off the trail to locate water. In any event, when they arrived at the site at dusk the water was there. His immediate reaction was "Praise the Lord." "It was pretty emotional," Jim said, "I didn't know I could get so excited over water!"

Those who hunger and thirst after righteousness do not need to worry about being left high and dry! If need be, God will provide streams in the desert. The prophet Isaiah declared the promise of God this way: "See, a king will reign in righteousness and rulers will rule with justice. Each person will be like a shelter from the wind and a refuge from the storm, like streams of water in the desert and the shadow of a great rock in a thirsty land" (Isaiah 32:1-2). The psalmist likens the person who delights in the law of the Lord, the person who implements, obeys, and puts the will of God into practice, to "a tree planted by streams of water, which yields its fruit in season and whose leaf does not wither" (Psalm 1:2-3).

The promise of God's provision found in the 23rd Psalm, "You prepare a table before me in the presence of my enemies," finds its ultimate fulfillment in the Eucharistic meal. Jesus took the bread, gave thanks and broke it, and said, "This is my body given for you; do this in remembrance of me." And he took the cup, saying, "This cup is the new covenant in my blood, which is poured out for you" (Luke 22:19-20). Therefore whenever we "eat this bread and drink this cup, [we] proclaim the Lord's death until he comes" (1 Corinthians 11:26). God's provision is complete in Christ and meets all of our needs – body, mind and soul. "For the bread of God is he who comes down from heaven and gives life to the world" (John 6:33). Everyone who gathers around this table, which Christ prepares in the presence of our enemies, ought to recognize the needs of the worldwide body of Christ, and hunger and thirst for righteousness (1 Corinthians 11:29).

5 Showing Mercy

*"Blessed are the merciful,
for they will be shown mercy."*

Matthew 5:7

The British preacher, Martyn Lloyd-Jones, emphasized that the beatitudes were not independent sayings but interdependent summations.[39] Each beatitude illuminates the others and together they reflect a comprehensive picture of the follower of the Lord Jesus Christ. The first four beatitudes describe our need before God. To be poor in spirit is to acknowledge our dependence upon God. To mourn is to grieve over our sin and repent before God. To be meek is to submit to the will of God in everything. To hunger and thirst for righteousness is to seek after God's justice in every area of life. Starting over and moving forward in the Jesus way impacts our relationship with God and with one another.

The next four beatitudes describe our response to others in the light of the first four beatitudes. We show mercy to our neighbor because we are completely dependent on the mercy of God. We are fully devoted to God with integrity and an undivided heart because we are sensitive to our sin and comforted by his forgiveness. We are peacemakers because we are submissive to the will of God. We suffer persecution for Christ's sake because we seek first His kingdom and His righteousness. Taken in this way, the beatitudes hold up a picture before the disciple and the world of what it means to belong to the Body of Christ. This is what membership in the

Household of Faith was meant to look like in the real world. The question before us is, what does it mean to be merciful?

Of all the beatitudes the fifth beatitude may appear the most obvious. Just about everyone feels they have a fairly good idea of what mercy is and for the most part they hope they are merciful. On the surface, Jesus appears to be giving a simple equation: You have to show mercy to receive mercy. Expressed as a simple moral aphorism, a quid-pro-quo exchange, it could have been said by Buddha or Confucius or Benjamin Franklin or Oprah. Any moral instructor, spiritual director, or mentor could have said what Jesus said word for word, but would they have meant what Jesus meant? When it comes to showing mercy, are we fulfilling Jesus' expectations or our own?

The Meaning of Mercy

By this time it is clear that the beatitudes are subject to serious misinterpretation if we base their meaning on culture's definition of such things as mourning, meekness and mercy. Many people associate mercy with being easy-going, sensitive, and tolerant. Some interpret mercy as overextending oneself in good deeds. The merciful are congenial, charitable, kind, and considerate of other people's feelings. When mercy is thought of in this way, it is an attribute that suits some temperaments better than others. It appears to belong in a personality profile under "feelings" and whoever shows mercy is identified as a true people person. He or she loves to be accepting, caring and helpful. The problem with defining mercy as goodwill and a positive disposition toward others is that it substitutes a complimentary view of mercy for what Jesus meant by mercy. The popularly conceived view of mercy is a weak version of the real thing. It substitutes tolerance for truth, sensitivity for sacrifice, and a helpful attitude for deliberate, costly action. Mercy is anything but easy-going tolerance and a soft touch.

Biblical mercy does not depend on humanistic graciousness but on God's grace. It is not based on temperament, but on truth. When Jesus asked his disciples, "Who do people say that I am?" He received a stream of complimentary answers: "Some say John the Baptist; others say Elijah; and still others, Jeremiah or one of the prophets." In the popular imagination, Jesus could not have been thought of more highly, but even such high praise falls far short of his true identity. Then he asked, "Who do you say I am?" and Peter answered, "You are the Christ, the Son of the living God" (Matthew 16:13-16). The difference between the complimentary views of Jesus and Peter's Spirit-inspired confession of the Lord Jesus illustrates the difference between mercy, as it is popularly conceived, and mercy as Jesus commended it.

If we show the kind of mercy Jesus intended, two important things must happen. We will pay attention to the source of mercy and we will hear the cry for mercy. It is vital that we realize that mercy, like holiness, righteousness and justice, is an attribute of God and meaningless apart from God. If we disconnect mercy from its source in God, we rob mercy of its meaning. Mercy is to God what *The Magic Flute* is to Mozart or *Your Cheatin' Heart* is to Hank Williams. Think of mercy as God's definitive composition. Mercy is first and foremost, especially and specifically, a Divine attribute, and only secondarily a human quality. Wherever real mercy is shown, it belongs to God and is derived from God. Paul's salutation says it succinctly, "Grace, mercy and peace from God the Father and Christ Jesus our Lord" (2 Timothy 1:2).

When Moses sought reassurance of God's presence and promise, he asked to see God's glory. The Lord said, "I will cause all my goodness to pass in front of you, and I will proclaim my name, the Lord, in your presence. I will have mercy on whom I will have mercy, and I will have compassion on whom I will have compassion" (Exodus 33:19). The qualities of goodness, mercy and compassion, which are identified in God's self-revelation to Moses, underscore God's care for people who are in desperate need. Mercy is God's exclusive prerogative and humankind's absolute need. The biblical meaning of mercy goes to the heart of the human dilemma. We need mercy, not random acts of human kindness, but radical divine redemption.

The tax collector in Jesus' parable said what every man, woman and child ought to express deeply, "God, have mercy on me, a sinner" (Luke 18:13). All the religion in the world, as the proud, self-righteous Pharisee illustrated, does not change the fact that God's mercy rather than human merit is our only hope for salvation. This is why the apostle Paul said, after quoting the all-important truth in Exodus 33 ("I will have mercy on whom I have mercy, and will have compassion on whom I have compassion"), that salvation does not depend upon human desire or effort, "but on God's mercy" (Romans 9:16). "He saved us," declared Paul, "not because of righteous things we had done, but because of his mercy" (Titus 3:5).

This truth helps us see that God's mercy is fundamentally defined by his saving grace. The exhortation in Hebrews makes this clear, "Let us then approach the throne of grace with confidence, so that we may receive mercy and find grace to help us in our time of need" (Hebrews 4:16). As does Peter's doxology, "Praise be to the God and Father of our Lord Jesus Christ! In his great mercy he has given us new birth into a living hope through the resurrection of Jesus Christ from the dead..." (1 Peter 1:3).

Throughout the Bible the cry for mercy is directed to the Lord God, who is the sole source from which all mercy flows. The psalmist's repeated cries to God for mercy serve as a constant reminder of our many and varied needs and of God's gracious provision: "Hear my cry for mercy as I call to you for help, as I lift up my hands toward your Most Holy Place" (Psalm 28:2); "Have mercy on me, O Lord, for I call to you all day long... Hear my prayer, O Lord; listen to my cry for mercy... Turn to me and have mercy on me..." (Psalm 86:3,6,16); "O Lord, hear my prayer, listen to my cry for mercy; in your faithfulness and righteousness come to my relief" (Psalm 143:1). Given the Old Testament emphasis on God as the source of all mercy, it is especially noteworthy that in the Gospels, the cry for mercy is directed to Jesus. Two blind men cried out, "Have mercy on us, Son of David!" (Matthew 9:27). A Canaanite woman approached Jesus on behalf of her demonized daughter, saying, "Lord, Son of David, have mercy on me!" (Matthew 15:22). Blind Bartimaeus shouted out, "Jesus, Son of David, have mercy on me!" (Mark 10:47).

Mercy takes on Jesus' intended meaning when we root its source in God and its purpose in meeting the full range of human needs, especially the need for forgiveness and reconciliation with God. Good commentators differ over their interpretation of mercy in the fifth beatitude. Some believe that Jesus is calling his followers to show compassion and kindness, while others stress that Jesus is calling his followers to commend the gospel of grace to all who are lost. The beauty of the biblical meaning of mercy is that it covers the full range of human need. It expresses compassion for the lost, as well as compassion for the hungry. The mercy of God addresses both our spiritual and physical needs in such a way as to respond to the fact that we are made in God's image. We are neither bodyless souls nor soulless bodies but bodies and souls in community. This is why we cannot separate ministries of compassion and ministries of evangelism.

Those who show mercy to others are people who have been transformed by God's mercy. They acknowledge their utter dependence upon God. They know that they are saved by God's grace alone, and that the evidence for being genuinely poor in spirit (the first beatitude) is to show mercy (the fifth beatitude). The reason they are merciful is because they live in awe of the God who has shown them mercy. "...The merciful are those who reflect God's acceptance of the unworthy, the guilty, and the ones in the wrong, because they have received mercy themselves. They are conscious of their own unworthiness, guilt, and wrong and have experienced God's forgiving and restoring acceptance through the message of Jesus Christ. There is often a unique feeling of understanding, a healing rapport, between those sharing a common trauma. This common bond can serve as a basis for conduct."[40]

Those who are deeply moved by the mercy of God have a deep affinity for those in need of God's mercy. This is why the apostle Paul challenged us "in view of God's mercy," to offer our bodies as living sacrifices (Romans 12:1). David Mensah, an African brother from Ghana, exemplifies the passion to be merciful in response to the mercy he has received from God. My wife Virginia remembers the time in Toronto when she offered David a glass of cold water and he started to cry. This was in the early 1980's and back home in his village in northern Ghana, people were dying from starvation and drought. Women were having to walk for miles to get water. Inspired by the grace and mercy of Christ, David committed himself to showing his people the mercy of God. In the years since, wells have been dug, the gospel preached, children taught, schools built, land cultivated, crops planted, animals raised, widows fed, medical clinics opened, and churches planted. The work of God's mercy continues through David and a team of committed brothers and sisters in Christ.

German theologian and martyr, Dietrich Bonhoeffer, offered a moving description of those who show mercy: "These are men and women without possessions or power, these strangers on earth, these sinners, these followers of Jesus, have in their life with him renounced their own dignity, for they are merciful.... They have an irresistible love for the downtrodden, the sick, the wretched, the wronged, the outcast and all who are tortured with anxiety.... For the only honor and dignity they know is their Lord's own mercy, to which alone they owe their very lives."[41] Until we can honestly say we have experienced the mercy of God, I am not sure we can understand the meaning of mercy, let alone show mercy.

Parables on Mercy

Jesus used two parables to give the best illustrations for the wideness of God's mercy. He told the Parable of the Unmerciful Servant (Matthew 18:21-35) in response to Peter's question, "Lord, how many times shall I forgive my brother when he sins against me? Up to seven times?" Jesus responded, "I tell you, not seven times, but seventy-seven times." His message in response to Peter and in the story that follows is that God's mercy extended to us exceeds anything we could possibly show to others. As the apostle Paul said, "Bear with each other and forgive whatever grievances you may have against one another. Forgive as the Lord forgave you" (Colossians 3:13).

In the parable, Jesus said the kingdom of heaven is like a king settling accounts with his servants. The story line is normal enough, but everything else in the story is extreme. The first servant in line has an astronomical debt of ten thousand talents, which is like saying he owes the equivalent of the national debt! We are hardly exaggerating when we say this because "Herod's total annual income amounted to only nine hundred talents, and the taxes imposed on Galilee and Perea together only two hundred."[42] The size of the debt is indicative of gross corruption and indulgence on the scale of a Saddam Hussein or Liberian dictator Charles Taylor, and the king responds by ordering the confiscation of his entire family and all his possessions. The servant immediately fell to his knees and begged for mercy, saying, "Be patient with me and I will pay back everything." Jesus continued the story in a matter-of-fact tone, "The servant's master took pity on him, canceled the debt and let him go." One can only imagine the reaction of his hearers: "Yeah, right. Just like that, the king cancels the debt and lets him go. We've never heard of any king like that!" But Jesus isn't through with his story.

The servant, who has just been forgiven this staggering sum, leaves the presence of the king only to run into a fellow servant who owes him a small amount of money. He grabs this poor guy by the throat and shouts, "Pay back what you owe me!" The bullied servant fell to his knees and begged the unmerciful servant with the exact same words the unmerciful servant had used before the king, "Be patient with me, and I will pay you back." But the servant who had been forgiven an impossible debt and blessed beyond his wildest dreams, refused and threw his fellow servant into prison until he could pay the debt. When news of this got back to the king he summoned the unmerciful servant and confronted him, saying, "You wicked servant. I cancelled all that debt of yours because you begged me to. Shouldn't you have had mercy on your fellow servant just as I had on you?" In anger, the king had him thrown into jail "until he should pay back all he owed." Then Jesus said, "This is how my heavenly Father will treat each of you unless you forgive your brother and sister from your heart" (Matthew 18:35).

The message is simple: the boundless grace of God knows no limits. No debt of sin, no matter how great, is too great for the mercy of God to forgive.[43] Those who have received God's mercy will naturally and easily show God's mercy to those who ask for forgiveness. To do otherwise is to despise God's mercy and call down judgment on ourselves.

The parable argues against the logic that makes showing

mercy to others a condition for receiving God's mercy. It is the other way around. Whatever mercy we show to others comes as a result of the mercy God has shown to us. Our forgiveness of others is always based on God's forgiveness of us. If it was not this way "it is very certain that not one of us would be forgiven and not one of us would see heaven."[44] God's *mercy* far surpasses anything we deserve and comes before God's *demand* which expects from us far, far less than we have already received. God's mercy precedes everything else and everything we do is done in the light of Christ and his Cross.[45] When we pray, "Forgive us our debts as we have forgiven our debtors," we are not turning the gospel upside down and basing divine forgiveness on the human capacity to forgive. We are not implying that if we forgive others we have earned the right to be forgiven by God.[46] On the contrary, we are acknowledging that God's forgiveness of our sins inspires our forgiveness of others. To be forgiven by God is to be forgiving of others. "You can't get forgiveness from God, without also forgiving others. If you refuse to do your part, you cut yourself off from God's part." Therefore, we pray, "Keep us forgiven with you and forgiving others" (Matthew 6:12,14-15, The Message).

In the parable of the Good Samaritan, Jesus extends the mercy of forgiveness to the mercy of compassion and shows us the full range of mercy. The parable was prompted by a teacher of the law who was hoping to justify himself (Luke 10:25-37). The expert in the law wanted a legal formula that limited the obligation of neighbor-love. His insight into the essence of the law was right on: "Love the Lord your God with all your heart and with all your soul and with all your strength and with all your mind," followed by, "Love your neighbor as yourself." And Jesus replied positively, "You have answered correctly. Do this and you will live." But the teacher of the law wasn't satisfied. The idea of loving one's neighbor without legal boundaries seemed too open-ended and vague. "It is really very awkward and annoying that spiritual things should be so simple," writes Helmut Thielicke, "that they should have to do with ridiculous everyday life, with neighbors, friends, retailers, or any insignificant, colorless employee who happens to come along."[47] But the expert in the law wanted boundaries and definable goals. He wanted to be practical and reasonable about neighbor-love. He must have thought to himself, "Surely I can't be expected to love everybody as myself."

If we're honest, we can see ourselves asking the same question. Like him, we want to feel good about ourselves. We want to feel that we are doing our fair share and that anything more would seem excessive. We already feel bombarded by overwhelming needs from every quarter. Compassion fatigue is a real danger. The teacher's question makes sense. Let's draw boundaries and limit our liability. "Jesus, we need you to define 'neighbor.'" Yet it is hard to be honest when what we are looking for is a loophole.

Instead of giving the man what he wanted, a well-worded formula that limited the extent of neighbor-love, he told him a story that opened up possibilities that he never dreamed of. Jesus could have told him to color within the lines, but instead he erased the very lines that any self-respecting Jew counted on. Under the guise of being practical, the teacher wanted to talk about loving his neighbor in the abstract. But by telling the story of one man who was mugged and left for half dead, Jesus addressed the issue practically and personally. The true humanitarian does not work in generalities but in specifics. He or she knows that when the subject is humankind in general the individual person gets lost in the discussion. The expert in the law wanted to talk about policy and Jesus wanted to talk about a single, individual person. The whole discussion changed from theory to practice when Jesus began, "A man was going down from Jerusalem to Jericho..." Jesus goes on to describe the victim as having been robbed so thoroughly and beaten so badly that he was stripped of all identifying marks that might have helped the priest and Levite to identify his social and cultural background. The robbers had not only stolen his clothes and destroyed his body, they had also, from a human point of view, taken away his identity. The teacher wanted Jesus to limit the identity of his neighbor, but Jesus refused to do this. By telling the story the way he did, he intentionally removed the everyday social indicators and cultural symbols that people often use to determine who they are willing to relate to. For Jesus the real issue of neighbor-love involved a single person in great need, no matter what his cultural identity was. The startling twist to the story comes, however, when Jesus put the cultural indicators back into the story by identifying a priest, a Levite, and a Samaritan traveler.

Knowing as we do that the religious leaders felt antagonistic toward Jesus, we might be tempted to misunderstand why Jesus used a priest and a Levite to describe those who saw the victim and passed by on the other side. Given our sensitivity to religious hypocrisy and disingenuous church leaders, most people today would not identify themselves with the priest or Levite. However when Jesus told the story he expected his hearers to identify with the priest and Levite as the very ones who were the most respected for obeying the law and loving their neighbor.

The crux of the story revolves around the fact that the esteemed law keepers did nothing for the man and the despised Samaritan did everything he could for the man. Healthy self-esteem, a busy schedule, a good education and respecting people like ourselves, may do wonders for our self-image and yet very little for showing mercy. It takes somebody who knows what it is like to be despised, to feel pity and respond with compassion. Those who think they have merited their place in life despise those who need mercy, whereas those who know they need mercy are the ones who show mercy.

Jesus painted a beautiful picture of the Samaritan's compassion. First he saw the man, but unlike the priest and Levite, he did not pass by on the other side. Instead, he "took pity on him" and "he went to him" and he cleaned, disinfected, and bandaged the man's wounds. Then he lifted the man up onto his own donkey and took him to an inn where he cared for him. Having done all he could for the man, he left on his journey, but not before covering the cost of the man's recuperation. Martyn Lloyd-Jones describes mercy as "pity plus action" and the good Samaritan could not have illustrated it better. Mercy is "an inward sympathy and outward acts in relation to the sorrows and sufferings of others."[48]

At the end of the story, Jesus asked the teacher, "Which of these three do you think was a neighbor to the man who fell into the hands of robbers?" The expert in the law answered, "The one who had mercy on him." Note the turn in logic. Instead of asking whether the victim qualified as a neighbor, Jesus asked him who was a neighbor to the victim. The question is not who is my neighbor but whether I am willing to be a neighbor. The question is not who has the right to be a burden to me, but to whom do I have the privilege of being a blessing? The Law limits my liability, but Grace liberates my love. That is why the apostle Paul said, after describing the fruit of the Spirit, "against such there is no law" (Galatians 5:23). Showing mercy is not a meritorious duty, but a free and liberating act of devotion. If I am willing to be a neighbor, I don't have to ask who is my neighbor. Those who have received God's mercy take delight in showing mercy to others, because they know that if this mercy were predicated on anything other than God's mercy for us, it would be an impossible burden. It is only by God's grace that Jesus can say to us, "Be merciful, just as your Father is merciful" (Luke 6:36).

Love Mercy

One hears Christians say that if they only knew what God wanted them to do they would do it. I have heard believers complain that they don't know what the goals of the church are and they don't know where to fit in. Some even act as if it is a conspiracy on the part of church leadership to leave them out of the game. The danger, particularly in the middle class church, is to satisfy this desire with religious things to do: programs, meetings, committees and events. Many people are more than willing to knock themselves out performing for Jesus. But is this what Jesus wants? When the prophet Micah asked the question, "And what does the Lord require of you?" he did so after listing some of the possibilities that readily fill the religious imagination. He sarcastically referred to outward displays of religion, impressive offerings, special performances, and heroic sacrifices. But the prophet insisted that this is not what the Lord wanted and that the Lord had already shown them what he wanted: "To act justly, to love mercy and to walk humbly with your God" (Micah 6:8).

The God of all mercy has called us to love mercy and to reach out to a lost world with his compassion and forgiveness. When Jesus was criticized for showing mercy to "tax collectors and sinners," he answered back, saying, "It is not the healthy who need a doctor, but the sick. But go and learn what this means: 'I desire mercy, not sacrifice.' For I have not come to call the righteous, but sinners" (Matthew 9:12-13).

6 Purifying the Heart

*"Blessed are the pure in heart,
for they will see God."*

Matthew 5:8

The beatitudes describe a state of grace, a life fully alive by the grace of our Lord Jesus Christ. Embedded in these eight one-line summations is the interpretative key for the whole Sermon on the Mount. And together they provide a compelling picture of how grace renovates the heart and transforms life. Extracted from the whole counsel of God and the Master who declared them, they are only tag lines, meaning whatever the hearer wants them to mean. But because they are deeply rooted in the meaning of the Old Testament and modeled in the life of the Savior, each deftly expresses in a single line the essence of what it means to follow Christ.

The meaning of the sixth beatitude has its roots in the majestic 24th Psalm. True worshipers "ascend" into the presence of the Lord of Creation, who is Holy and Almighty, with "clean hands and a pure heart." The ascent implies "a deliberate quest."[49] Nothing else matters. Worship involves an all-absorbing purpose, vision and passion, signified by both outward preparation ("clean hands") and inward purification ("a pure heart"). Nothing is allowed to distract from the worshiper's singular purpose, neither visible idols nor false motivations. The benefits are not man-made but totally God given. "He will receive blessing from the Lord and vindication from God his Savior. Such is the generation of those who seek him, who seek your face, O God of Jacob" (Psalm 24:5-6). The all-pervading presence of the King of Glory calls for the purity of heart that wills one thing: to worship God wholeheartedly with our whole being.

Purity of Heart

Blessed are the pure in heart. The heart symbolizes who we are in the depth of our being, both positively and negatively. We are commanded to love the Lord our God with all our heart, and with all our soul and with all our strength (Deuteronomy 6:5). Yet we are told by the prophet Jeremiah that "the heart is deceitful above all things and beyond cure" (Jeremiah 17:9). Jesus said, "For out of the heart come evil thoughts, murder, adultery, sexual immorality, theft, false testimony, slander" (Matthew 15:19; see Luke 6:45). Yet it is with the heart that we believe and are justified, and it is with the mouth that we confess and are saved (Romans 10:10). David had a heart after God's own heart (Acts 13:22) and the hardhearted Israelites were said to have a "heart of stone" (Ezekiel 36:26). Real wisdom is trusting in the Lord with all your heart and leaning not on your own understanding (Proverbs 3:5). Throughout the Old Testament the people of God are exhorted to serve the Lord with all their heart and soul (Deuteronomy 10:12; Joshua 22:5). True communication means speaking the truth from the heart (Psalm 15:2), because the message has been taken to heart (Revelation 1:3), even as true counsel instructs the heart (Psalm 16:7). True repentance is "a broken and contrite heart" (Psalm 51:17; see Joel 2:13; Romans 2:29). Real maturity is characterized by having "integrity of heart" (Psalm 70:72), "an undivided heart" (Psalm 86:11), "an upright heart" (Psalm 119:7), a "singleness of heart" (Jeremiah 32:39), a humble heart (Matthew 11:29), a "heart of wisdom" (Psalm 90:12), and a "sincere heart in full assurance of faith" (Hebrews 10:22).

Only the Lord really knows the heart. The psalmist prays, "May the words of my mouth and the meditation of my heart be pleasing in your sight, O Lord, my Rock and my Redeemer" (Psalm 19:14). "Test me, O Lord, and try me," David prayed, "examine my heart and my mind; for your love is ever before me, and I walk continually in your truth" (Psalm 26:2-3). What we are like outwardly may be a charade. The real issue is a person's heart, which has a way of showing its true colors under the pressure of time and circumstance. As the psalmist prayed, "Surely you desire truth in the inner self; you teach wisdom in the inmost place" (Psalm 51:6).

Things are not always as they appear. Recently I was waiting in line in a sandwich shop when I noticed a young guy ahead of me who looked like he was poor and possibly homeless. His jeans were old and torn as was his T-shirt and he had one of those John Deere baseball caps pulled down on a pile of unkept curly hair. I expected him to ask me for some money because he kept glancing over at me. I was trying to decide whether I should give him something if he asked. Imagine my surprise when he picked up an unusual large order and jumped into a Porsche parked by the front entrance. When I shared this with our daughter she asked me if I had looked at the clothes for sale at Abercrombie & Fitch lately.

If judging appearances is difficult, how much more the heart? This is why David prayed, "Search me, O God, and know my heart: test me and know my anxious thoughts" (Psalm 139:23). Only the Lord can search the heart and examine the mind (Jeremiah 17:10) and only the word of God can truly discern "the thoughts and attitudes of the heart" (Hebrews 4:12).

In conversation with a university professor who has spent his career studying the insurance industry, and in the process, honed the art of precise prose, said to me that he found the term "heart" confusing and misleading. He did not see what the physical organ or romantic sentiment had to do with the

Christian life. Yet the heart is an uncontested biblical and cultural metaphor for who we are and who we are becoming. I have sent many cards and letters over the years to my wife affirming my love for her "with all my heart." Never once has Virginia sent one of the letters back with "heart" circled and a question mark added, wondering what I meant by "all my heart."

By interpreting the sixth beatitude in the light of Psalm 24 and by understanding the metaphor of the heart we avoid drawing the unwarranted conclusion that Dallas Willard has about this beatitude. Instead of identifying the pure in heart with those who are honest and transparent before God, Willard associates this "purity" with hypocrisy and perfectionism. These are "the ones for whom nothing is good enough, not even themselves..."

> *"They are a pain to everyone, themselves most of all. In religion they will certainly find errors in your doctrine, your practice, and probably your heart and your attitude. They may be even harder on themselves. They endlessly pick over their own motivations. They wanted Jesus to wash his hands even though they were not dirty and called him a glutton and winebiber. Their food is never cooked right; their clothes and hair are always unsatisfactory; they can tell you what is wrong with everything. How miserable they are!"*[50]

Willard interprets this beatitude as if it had been given by a Pharisee instead of by Jesus. He reacts as if it were a self-righteous claim to purity, steeped in hypocrisy, instead of a call for undivided devotion to God, encouraging honesty and transparency from the inside out. As in Psalm 24, the challenge to be pure in heart is neither humanistic nor legalistic, but is inspired and empowered by the majesty of God and *his grace*. What is important to realize is that to be pure in heart is not puritanical extremism. It is not something that super religious types aspire to. On the contrary, it is a key description of the ordinary follower of Jesus. The metaphor of the heart corrects any misunderstanding that we might have that would associate "purity" with ceremonial cleansing, outward conformity and performance perfectionism. Martin Luther understood what Jesus was saying when he wrote, "Christ...wants to have the heart pure, though outwardly the person may be a drudge in the kitchen, black, sooty, and grimy, doing all sorts of dirty work."[51]

Double-mindedness

Jesus identified the pure in heart by deliberately drawing on the language of Psalm 24. The purity of heart that he had in mind was not primarily sexual purity, although sexual purity is certainly included, but he thought of a whole life of single-minded devotion. If the soul rejects all idols, then the true inner self, the real you, that is, the vital, living being of the person, the center of emotion, desire, intelligence, memory and passions, rejects everything that interferes, evades, subverts and distracts from pure devotion to God. And if the person refuses to swear by what is false it means that all deception, cleverness, manipulation, flattery and flippancy are rejected in favor of truth, clarity, integrity, and honesty. Commitment and confession line-up together and the outer life is consistent with the interior life. Devotion to God is from the heart, rather than a performance to be seen by others.

Purity of heart relates to virtually every issue covered in the Sermon on the Mount because it goes to the core of our relationship to God. Our honesty and transparency before God is critical to determining our ambition, vision and devotion in life. Materialism is a purity of heart issue because, "where your treasure is, there your heart will be also" (Matthew 6:21). Divided loyalties violate the purity of our hearts, because "no one can serve two masters" (Matthew 6:24). Worry and anxiety interfere with the purity of heart that seeks first Christ's Kingdom and his righteousness. The sixth beatitude is at the crux of every tension in the Sermon on the Mount between the way of the world and the way of Christ.

In his book *Purity of Heart* (1846), Soren Kierkegaard examined the spiritual direction given in James 4:8: "Come near to God and he will come near to you. Wash your hands, you sinners, and purify your hearts, you double-minded." He explored the professing believer's capacity to *evade* the purity of heart that wills one thing. Like a detective, Kierkegaard sought "to track down double-mindedness into its hidden ways and to ferret out its secret."[52] He exposed the "many errors, disappointments, deceptions, and self-deceptions" that hinder us from whole-hearted obedience to the will of God. Of course, the object of this single-minded devotion, which Kierkegaard sought to defend, was no "thing" at all, but God himself and God alone. To will the one thing necessary, was to will only the *Good*, which was Kierkegaard's way of saying *all that God wills*. He used the term "Good" as Jesus did with the rich young ruler, "No one is good—except God alone" (Luke 18:19). Kierkegaard's immediate concern was not outright disbelief or obvious worldliness or overt sin, but the more subtle forms of double-mindedness that afflict the well-meaning, sincere believer who tends to be unaware of the problem of double-mindedness. Kierkegaard diagnosed specific causes of double-mindedness, including the chaotic nature of modern life, with its competitive, clever, often conceited, consumer-oriented culture. It is easy to say "be not conformed to this world, but be transformed" while merrily accommodating to the spirit of the times.

Kierkegaard was a physician of the soul who specialized in detecting serious maladies in people who felt satisfied with their spiritual lives. His dense prose was not designed to be read easily and quickly. He meant for us to read his work slowly, with careful concentration and long pauses for reflection. Even in this he reminds me of a conscientious physician who refuses to give the patient a cursory examination, but insists on a careful and methodical physical in the privacy of an examination room without being hurried and hassled.

As far as Kierkegaard was concerned, his main mission, and the motive behind his method and message, was for his readers to get real with God. He wanted to draw out the individual, silent the incessant noise of the crowd, and make time for genuine confession and repentance. "This silence," Kierkegaard extolled, "is the simple festivity of the holy act of confession. For at dancing and festive occasions worldly judgment holds that the more musicians, the better. But when we are thinking of divine things, the deeper the stillness the better. When the wanderer comes away from the much-traveled noisy highway into places of quiet, then it seems to him (for stillness is impressive) as if he must examine himself, as he must speak out what lies hidden in the depths of his soul."[53] It is only "when the tumults of the whirling senses are over, when all becomes soberly quiet" that we can confront our ignorant refusal to will the one thing and our cleverness at evading the one thing necessary.[54]

The noisy crowd and the pressure of busyness are often undetected enemies of the undivided heart. Kierkegaard put it well when he said: "Double-mindedness dwells in the press of busyness.... There is neither time nor quiet to win the transparency that is indispensable if a person is to come to understand himself in willing one thing.... The press of busyness into which one steadily enters further and further, and the noise in which the truth continually slips more and more into oblivion, and the mass of connections, stimuli, and hindrances, these make it ever more impossible for one to win any deeper knowledge of himself."[55]

The impact of busyness is felt at increasingly younger

ages. It "reaches out seeking always to lay hold of ever-younger victims so that childhood or youth are scarcely allowed the quiet and the retirement in which the Eternal may unfold a divine growth."[56] Those who are busy always have plenty of time for "a multitude of excuses" and plenty of company in the "widespread practice of excusing," but they still retain a feeling for God and his will. "If someone should speak of the Good, especially if it were done in a poetical [entertaining] fashion, then he is quickly moved, easily stimulated to melt away in emotion."[57] However, this feeling for God's will does not translate well into doing God's will. It is the old problem of faith without works. "The double-minded one is wholly blind to the fact that at the very moment when he believes faith to have conquered in him, he has, precisely by his action, refuted this conviction."[58]

Against the chaos of modern life the Lord challenges us, "Be still and know that I am God" (Psalm 46:10). This may help us gain a greater appreciation for our times of loneliness, when we feel cut off from our friends and loved ones or when we feel that no one loves us. Being quiet and alone may serve to remind us, in a deep life-transforming way, that in the Lord we are never alone. When I had cancer surgery during my senior year of high school, my pastor gave me a simple framed line of calligraphy that quoted Luke's description of Jesus on the road to Emmaus. It read, "Jesus himself drew near and went with them" (Luke 24:15). In the hospital, I experienced the presence of God in a way that is hard to put into words. This was also the case when I lived in Chung Li, Taiwan, for eight months. I felt very isolated and far from home, but my relationship to the Lord acquired new strength and meaning. When we are cut off from our normal routines we have the opportunity to examine the subtle and not so subtle forces that divide our hearts. Kierkegaard's calling was to make us aware of the forces that hinder our devotion to Christ.

The Unholy Enthusiast

The double-minded person suffers from the tyranny of many things at the expense of the one thing. Such a person feels pulled in a thousand directions. He or she is pressured to satisfy the tyranny of the urgent and practice the perfectionism of small things. The multiplicity of good things and the variety of great moments seduces the double-minded enthusiast into thinking that there are many things to choose from in life, when in fact, there is but one thing. Kierkegaard had no patience with the believer who thought that God's will was a confusing array of options. He held a very different vision:

> "In a certain sense nothing can be spoken of so briefly as the Good, when it is well described. For the Good without condition and without qualification, without preface and without compromise is, absolutely the only thing that a person may and should will, and is only one thing. Oh, blessed brevity, oh, blessed simplicity, that seizes swiftly what cleverness, tired out in the service of vanity, may grasp but slowly! That which a simple soul, in the happy impulse of a pious heart, feels no need of understanding in an elaborate way, since he or she simply seizes the Good immediately, is grasped by the clever one only at the cost of much time and much grief."[59]

Remember Mary and Martha's response to Jesus when he came for dinner? Martha did many good things, but Mary did only one thing. Martha opened her home, made preparations and tried to recruit Mary, who "sat at the Lord's feet listening to what he said" (Luke 10:40). Jesus did not compliment Martha for doing many things. Instead, he challenged her: "'Martha, Martha,' the Lord answered, 'you are worried and upset about many things, but only one thing is needed. Mary has chosen what is better, and it will not be taken away from her'" (Luke 10:41-42). Be on your guard, Kierkegaard warned of "the grave mistake of a brazen, unholy enthusiasm.... The enthusiast may swerve out of the true course and aim perhaps for the impressive instead of being led to the Good.... But God in heaven...does not reward the impressive with admiration."[60]

The only way we can check this unholy enthusiasm for life, which causes us to fall prey to the tyranny of the urgent and the perfectionism of small things, is by choosing the One thing. King David wrote, "One thing I ask of the Lord, this is what I seek: that I may dwell in the house of the Lord all the days of my life, to gaze upon the beauty of the Lord and seek him in his temple" (Psalm 27:4). The passion to worship God is the only thing that saves us from living dysfunctional and disoriented lives. "Failure to worship consigns us to a life of spasms and jerks, at the mercy of every advertisement, every seduction, every siren," writes Eugene Peterson. "Without worship we live manipulated and manipulating lives.... People who do not worship are swept into a vast restlessness, epidemic in the world, with no steady direction and no sustaining purpose."[61] But the purity of heart that wills one thing brings all of life into focus. It controls our fears, purifies our hopes, directs our energies and calms our souls.

The Religious Consumer

Kierkegaard's critique of modern life exposed the ulterior motives that people bring to their relationship with Christ. The double-minded person does not seek the will of God for its own sake but for a worldly reward. Today's consumer of religious experience renegotiates Jesus' promise of the abundant life to fit the American Dream. But a faith driven by ulterior motives and an incentive plan hardly fits with the purity of heart that wills one thing. "If a man loves a girl for the sake of her money," Kierkegaard asked, "who will call him a lover? He does not love the girl, but the money. He is not a lover but a money seeker."[62]

The double-minded are fine with the apostle's bold statement that "nothing will separate us from the love of God that is in Christ Jesus" as long as it is considered *sentimentally*. But the apostle Paul was not writing a Hallmark card! If the consequence for willing the one thing were persecution rather than success, and ridicule rather than respect, then the double-minded would be reluctant to even consider it. Kierkegaard reminds us that "here on earth" seeking God's will "is often temporarily rewarded by ingratitude, by lack of appreciation, by poverty, by contempt, by many sufferings, and now and then by death."[63]

Now more than ever it is important that the purity of heart that wills one thing be distinguished from an incentive package designed to appeal to the modern day religious consumer. Today's consummate consumer comes to church looking for professional child care, fully staffed Christian education departments, excellent music, exciting youth programs, a dynamic singles ministry, plenty of parking and convenient service times. The modern consumer is conditioned to look for the best possible deal for the lowest possible price. Given this pervasive consumer orientation, the critical question is, how materialistic does the church have to become to be spiritually effective? Put conversely, to what degree is the church to be counter cultural, bucking consumerism for the sake of the kingdom of God? Should we not challenge the dehumanizing power of consumerism? The church that tries to impress the world falls into the temptation of trying to prove its identity by changing stones to bread and ends up changing wine to water.

We need to ask if we are catering to connoisseurs of religious experience who value their freedom of choice and personal tastes at the expense of long-term commitment to the Body of Christ? Are we reaching the unchurched or unchurching the churched?[64] Instead of promising strategies that will make people's marriages happier and their jobs more successful we may need to preach what Jesus said, "If anyone would come after me, he must deny himself and take up his cross daily and follow me. For whoever wants to save his life will lose it, but whoever loses his life for me will save it" (Luke 9:23-24). As Dietrich Bonhoeffer said, "When Jesus calls a person he bids him come and die." The high cost of appealing to the religious consumer must be exchanged for the high cost of devotion to Christ and obedience.

The Duty-Driven Disciple

Kierkegaard identified the fears that drive the double-minded person to pursue the will of God, not for its own sake, but out of fear of loss and a dreadful sense of duty. Such fear is not the fear of the Lord, which is the beginning of wisdom, nor the fear of "the One who can destroy both soul and body in hell" (Matthew 10:28). It is rather the humanistic, worldly fear that dwells in the heart of a person who is afraid life will not work out if he does what he really wants to do. It is the fear that makes people feel trapped in seeking the will of God, the fear that longs for the selfish freedom to do whatever we please. It is the fear that people with an undivided heart should not fear: "loss of money, loss of reputation, misjudgment by others, neglect, the world's judgment, the ridicule of fools, the laughter of the frivolous, the cowardly whining of consideration, the inflated triviality of the moment . . . "[65]

This is the fear of the elder son in the parable of the lost son, who felt he was his father's slave instead of his father's son. But the problem was not with the loving father who related to his older son with love and respect, but with the elder son. "'My son,' the father said, 'you are always with me, and everything I have is yours'" (Luke 15:31). This is the fear that blinds the believer to the love of his Heavenly Father and turns obedience into drudgery and faithfulness into resentment. Only God, not fear or duty or will power, can empower a person to desire to chose to honor and obey God alone.

The Self-Focused Disciple

We can identify the double-minded person who seeks to please God through his own pride and heroic efforts. Such a person wills the one thing with "heaven-storming pride."[66] "He wills that the Good shall triumph through *him*, that he shall be the instrument, be the chosen one."[67] He denies the gap between God's will and his perception of success and offers a "pretentiously plausible approximation" in place of God's will.[68] The double-minded person is impatient with the apparent slowness of God's victory and he confuses this impatience with "humble, obedient enthusiasm."[69] Kierkegaard warns that "this double-minded person is not so easily recognized," because he is impressive and heroic, willing to sacrifice all, "only he will not sacrifice himself in daily self-forgetfulness. This he fears to do."[70]

There are numerous incidents in the Bible that illustrate the tendency to turn the work of God into our own work. Moses was unable to enter the Promised Land because he struck the rock in anger even though God had explicitly commanded that he speak to the rock (Numbers 20). King Saul was removed from office because he usurped the prophet's authority. Out of fear of losing control of his troops, he proceeded to offer sacrifices instead of waiting for Samuel (1 Samuel 13). Uzzah lost his life because of his irreverent act. He took hold of the Ark of the Covenant when the oxen transporting it stumbled. This act alone provoked the Lord's anger against him and he was immediately struck dead (2 Samuel 6). David's insistence on counting the fighting men of Israel and Judah resulted in a plague that killed seventy thousand people (1 Chronicles 21).

These incidents remain obscure and inscrutable to us apart from the sinful human tendency to assert its own will, and God's expressed concern that we remain stewards of His work, rather than becoming our own masters.

Judas was an extreme example of this presumptuousness. Although Judas was intimately connected to Jesus, he was "scandalized" by Jesus' path to the cross and "treacherously" wished to bring about what he thought was best. Kierkegaard claimed that such a person revels in the moment, but "fears that the course of time will reveal his double-mindedness.... He is a falsifier. For him, eternity is the deceptive sensory illusion of the horizon..."[71] It is inevitable that a deep chasm opens up between heroic enthusiasm and humble obedience. God "puts on the slowness of time as a poor garment, and in keeping with this change of dress one who serves it must be clothed in the insignificant figure of the unprofitable servant. With the eye of his senses he is not permitted to see the Good in victory. Only with the eye of faith can he strive after its eternal victory."[72]

The best counsel that we can give to anyone who seeks to please the Lord is the reminder that "*it is not about you.*" Self-focused disciples make too much of their feelings, emotions, sacrifices and decisions. It is as if the ministry revolves around them. Unwittingly they over-interpret the sixth beatitude.

The problem of being preoccupied with ourselves means that we make life unnecessarily complicated. It is interesting to compare Elizabeth Elliot's *Shadow of the Almighty: The Life and Testament of Jim Elliot* with the correspondence between Dietrich Bonhoeffer and his fiance, Maria von Wedemeyer (1943-1945) published in *Love Letters From Cell 92*.

Jim Elliot struggled with how romantic love could be reconciled with the purity of heart that wills one thing. He marveled that a person "conquered by a power unseen, and willingly owning the sway of the Absolute," could "ache with a perfect fury to be subjugated still further to the rule of a woman's love." Jim Elliot put the two loves in tension:

> "Oh that Christ were All and Enough for me. He is supposed to be,...but oh, to be swept away in a flood of consuming passion for Jesus, that all desire might be sublimated to Him."[73]

Instead of seeing his love for Elizabeth as a gift from God he suspected that it might be a temptation. Early in their relationship he expressed his interest in her and shared a hymn by G. W. Frazer with her:

> Have I an object, Lord, below
> Which would divide my heart with Thee?
> Which would divert its own flow
> In answer to Thy constancy?
> O teach me quickly to return,
> And cause my heart afresh to burn.

Over time this became an agonizing concern for him. He was torn between his love for her and his love for the Lord and he saw these two loves in opposition. The tension was at times so great that he felt like a martyr. Even though he failed to receive his sought after sign from God that indicated marriage, he pursued her with intensity. He wrote to Elizabeth, "I will not say God is leading me to a life of celibacy. I only know what I need to know for now, and that is that the Lord does not want me seeking a wife until I have His definite sign. And apparently there is no immediate reason to expect that sign."

But after saying that he went on to describe how he had secretly fallen in love with her. "I can remember confessing to the Lord what I called 'my love for her,' and striving daily to forget and swallow hard. In those days of decision to keep silence, it seemed as if I had sealed the course of my whole life, and I must confess, I felt as if I were somewhat of a martyr."[74] On the one hand he wanted to continue writing but lurking in his mind was the possibility that God might say "no" and that "a more bitter renunciation" awaited them.[75]

For five years Jim struggled over whether marriage to Elizabeth was compatible with missionary service. He continued to be torn between his love for her and his passion to do God's will. At 25 he wrote, "Oh, what an ache wanting you can bring, when I knew that the wanting itself is good, right, even God-granted, but realize that now it is wisely God-denied, and that He has not let me know all the wisdom of the denial."[76] But then in January, 1953, he proposed to Elizabeth. He wrote to his parents, "I think I have the will of God on this. It has certainly not been done in a hurry, and the rest He has given in the matter since last fall has been a constant witness to the certainty of it."[77]

They were married on October 8, 1953, in a civil ceremony in Quito. He wrote to his parents five days earlier. "Nobody can accuse us of rushing things just because we have decided to get married in less than three weeks—we have been in love for over five years and I think considered the will of God in marriage as carefully as anyone could.... Few have really tried to understand our long waiting for engagement and my going to the jungle single. Few really thought we were the 'perfect match' in the first place.... 'They shall not be ashamed that wait for Me.'"[78]

The internal spiritual struggle that Jim Elliot faced over marriage may have been largely self-inflicted, born of a spirituality based more on subjective and intuitive biblical interpretation than on biblical-based theological truths. The biblical doctrines of God and the human person, sin and salvation, seem to be sublimated by a devotional reading of the Bible that considered a believer's existential experience more important than a Christian world-view. The hoped for sign never materialized but thankfully Jim had the good sense and peace of mind to accept Elizabeth as God's gracious provision for him and marry her. The story of their friendship and courtship raises important questions: How do we distinguish between a self-imposed burden and true obedience to the will of God? How does the principle of the "easy yoke" and the discipline of surrender relate to marriage and ministry?

There is a decidedly different spirit to the correspondence between Dietrich Bonhoeffer and his fiancé, Maria von Wedemeyer (1943-1945). Their letters are filled with a deep sense of mutual love. And even with Dietrich in prison and Maria suffering the loss of her father, her brother and two cousins in the war, there is a sense of God's great blessing in their lives. Maria writes affectionately, "My dear, dear Dietrich" and expresses her love with such self-less empathy and personal longing: "I never thought I could miss you and long for you more than I do, but I've done so twice as much since yesterday. You're right: one just can't imagine what a wedding means, however constantly one tries to live with the idea. What I myself have experienced and can truly understand—being utterly alone with one's personal experiences, sensing and grasping how powerless one's thoughts are—is such a small part of all that you are undergoing. If only I could see you once, however briefly!

"My dearest Dietrich, every morning at six, when we both fold our hands in prayer, we know that we can have great faith, not only in each other but far, far above and beyond that. And then you can't be sad any more either, can you?"

Bonhoeffer wrote to Maria from prison rejoicing in God's guidance (August 12, 1943):

"So now to your letter. You can't possibly imagine what it means to me, in my present predicament, to have you. I'm under God's special guidance here, I feel secure. To me, the way in which we found each other such a short time before my arrest seems a definite indication of that. Once again, things went 'according to man's confusion and God's providence.' It amazes me anew every day how little I have deserved such happiness, just as it daily and deeply moves me that God should have put you through such an ordeal this past year, and that he so clearly meant me to bring you grief and sorrow, so soon after we got to know each other, to endow our love with the proper foundation and proper strength. Moreover, when I consider the state of the world, the total obscurity enshrouding our personal destiny, and my present imprisonment, our union—if it wasn't frivolity, which it certainly wasn't—can only be a token of God's grace and goodness, which summon us to believe in him. We would have to be blind not to see that. When Jeremiah said, in his people's hour of direst need, that 'houses and fields and vineyards shall again be bought in this land' (Jeremiah 32:15), it was a token of confidence in the future. That requires faith, and may God grant it to us daily. I don't mean faith that flees the world, but the faith that endures *in* the world and loves and remains true to that world in spite of all the hardships it brings us. Our marriage must be a 'yes' to God's earth. It must strengthen our resolve to do and accomplish something on earth. I fear that Christians who venture to stand on earth on only one leg will stand in heaven on only one leg too....

"It's a cloudy, rainy day outside, a perfect accompaniment to my fruitless wait for the situation to resolve itself. But let us never forget how much we have to be thankful for, and how much good we experience even so; I have only to think of you, and all the little shadows on my soul disperse. So let us continue to be really patient for the rest of the time we're compelled to wait, and not waste a single hour grousing and grumbling. From God's standpoint, this time of waiting is immensely valuable; much depends on how we endure it and on whether we need not feel ashamed, later on, of having failed to recognize these months of testing as a gift from God. I'm convinced that our love and our marriage will derive eternal strength from this time of trial. So let us wait, with and for each other, until our wedding day dawns. It won't be much longer, my dear, dear Maria!..."[78]

Dietrich and Maria were not filled with anxiety over the tension between their love for one another and their love for the Lord. They experienced a calm assurance that God had providentially brought them together even though their life circumstances were filled with conflict and uncertainty. There was no self-imposed martyr complex or subjective interpretation of Scripture. Although their future was so uncertain their love for God and one another filled them with peace. They rested under the shadow of the Almighty.

It is important for all of us to remember that we are not the central characters even in our own life's story, let alone in God's salvation history story. This insight is not meant to demean us; it's meant to set us free. "It's not about you" is a powerful antidote to the well-intentioned, but misguided, self-focused disciple.[80]

Kierkegaard's critique of cultural Christianity exposed the dynamics of double-mindedness. He portrayed the unholy enthusiast, the religious consumer, the duty-driven disciple and the self-focused disciple in order that we might fix our eyes on Jesus.

To See God

What can we do to overcome the sin of double-mindedness and restore the purity of heart that wills to obey God with our whole being? The simple word *all* with its all-encompassing reality is the key. Unless we swallow the truth of this tiny word completely, we will never know the health and wholeness of an undivided heart. We will never truly see God.

The person who commits himself to this *all* cannot find time to do all things. "But neither does he need to do that, for he wills only one thing, and just on that account he will not have to do all possible things, and so he finds ample time for the Good."[81] Along with the apostle Paul, the pure in heart can do all things, but only those things that can be done through Christ who gives them strength (Philippians 4:13). Purity of heart means becoming all things to all people, "so that by all possible means I might save some." But what we become is all "for the sake of the gospel, that [we] may share in its blessings" (1 Corinthians 9:22-23).

This is the *all* that must not be evaded but embraced by all who desire to please God, because God's holy claim rests equally on all. As Kierkegaard said, "It makes no difference at all, God be praised, how great or how small the task may be. In relation to the highest of all this simply does not matter when it comes to being willing to do all. Oh, how great is the mercy of the Eternal toward us! All the ruinous quarreling and comparison which swells up and injures, which sighs and envies, the Eternal does not recognize.... The demand upon each is exactly the same: to be willing to do all."[82] It is not whether we do this or that, but whether we do all that God calls us to do. *We* put a certain premium on certain jobs and roles, but God does not.

This is the *all* that makes the all-important distinction between temporal and eternal achievements. Through cleverness, the double-minded person knows how to be very successful in the eyes of the world and achieve great things, but it is also the clever person who looks down on the poor widow described by Jesus who gave her all. The ingenious have no idea how God views her, because before God her gift was "as great a sum as all of the world's gold in a single heap, and if one who owned all the gold in the world gave it all, he would give no more."[83] In an effort "to accomplish all the more for the Good" the clever person evades the purity of God and the exclusiveness of his truth. "The clever one knows just how the Good must be altered a tiny particle in order to win the world's good will. He knows how much should be added to it and how much should be subtracted." And "the secret of deception" lies in the theory that it is not people who stand in the need of the Good, but the Good that stands in the need of people. "On that account it is people who must be won." And the clever try to win them adding "a little extra" and "eluding the Good a little."[84]

In their cleverness, people refuse to sell all and buy into the single investment that is priceless. They have yet to understand Jesus when he told the parable of the hidden treasure: "The kingdom of heaven is like treasure hidden in a field. When a man found it, he hid it again, and then in his joy went and sold all he had and bought that field" (Matthew 13:44).

This is the *all* that believes that Jesus accomplished *all* on the Cross. Judging from a worldly perspective, Jesus' life ended in tragic failure. His crucifixion was a political accident that might have turned out otherwise, an ironic twist of fate. If he had only been more politically astute and opportunistic he might have capitalized on his popularity. This is how the worldly order judges the crucified one, but "a distinction must be made between the momentary and the eternal view of the thing."[85] The Cross is at the center of a "battleground of the two interpretations of what is meant by 'accomplishing.'"[86] From the perspective of the moment, all was lost, hopelessly lost. Yet eternally understood, Jesus "had in the same moment accomplished all, and on that account said, with eternity's wisdom, 'It is finished.'"[87]

This is the *all* that is willing to *suffer all* for God. For how we suffer reveals the purity of heart that wills one thing in truth. True sufferers realize that they better understand the purposes of God by experiencing pain and suffering than observing success and achievement. There is no whining, no deceitful evasion, no disappointment with God, and no acceptance of deliverance on the world's terms, "because to take one's suffering to heart is to be weaned from the temporal order, and from cleverness and from excuses, and from clever men and women and from anecdotes about this and that, in order to find rest in the blessed trustworthiness of the Eternal."[88] Real sufferers take up their cross and follow Jesus. They want "to know Christ and the power of his resurrection and the fellowship of sharing in his sufferings, becoming like him in his death, and so, somehow, to attain to the resurrection from the dead" (Philippians 3:10). True sufferers model themselves after the apostles, who "left the Sanhedrin rejoicing because they had been counted worthy of suffering disgrace for the Name" (Acts 5:41).

This is the *all* of a covenant love (as opposed to a contractual obligation) that is grandly inclusive of all we are and will be. The pure in heart pledge themselves in an all-encompassing, timeless commitment. "As long as our lives should last" is the bottom line of a costly vow that carries us all the way to Eternity. The purity of heart that wills one thing covenants to love Christ and serve him, worship and cherish him in prosperity and in adversity; in sorrow and in happiness; in sickness and in health; and forsaking all others, be united to him for all eternity.

This is the *all* that knows no limits. "There is a time for everything and a season for every activity under heaven," but this is the one thing for all time and the one thing upon which everything else depends for time and eternity. King David expressed his heartfelt longing when he said, "One thing I ask of the Lord, this is what I seek: that I may dwell in the house of the Lord *all the days of my life*, to gaze upon the beauty of the Lord and to seek him in his temple" (Psalm 27:4). This is the *all* that gives light to our vision of God. Without it we are in darkness, but with it everything is brought into the light.

Father in Heaven! What are we without You! What is all this human knowledge, vast accumulation though it be, but a chipped fragment if we do not know You! What is all this striving, even if it could rule the world, but a half-finished work if we do not know You: You the One, who art one thing and who art all!

So may You give to the intellect, wisdom to comprehend that one thing; to the heart, sincerity to receive this understanding; to the will, purity that wills one thing. In prosperity may You grant perseverance to will one thing; amid distractions, concentration to will one thing; in suffering, patience to will one thing. Oh, You who gives both the beginning and the completion, may You early, at the dawn of the day, give to the young person the resolution to will one thing. As the day wanes, may You give to the old person a renewed remembrance of his first resolution, that the first may be like the last, the last like the first, in possession of a life that has willed only one thing.[89]

Pursuing Peace

*"Blessed are the peacemakers,
for they will be called the sons of God."*

Matthew 5:9

The unique and distinctive character of the seventh beatitude is best understood in the light of the six previous beatitudes. Peacemaking is the natural pursuit of those who live in dependence upon the Lord and in anticipation of the Kingdom of God. We realize that in and of ourselves we have no peace. We depend upon his blessing, as the apostle Paul prayed, "May the God of hope fill you with all joy and peace as you trust in him, so that you may overflow with hope by the power of the Holy Spirit" (Romans 15:13). Peacemaking depends upon the divine promise, "You will keep in perfect peace him whose mind is steadfast, because he trusts in you" (Isaiah 26:3).

Six Prerequisites for Peacemaking

The first beatitude reminds us that peace is *a gift from God*. The second beatitude teaches that peace *with* God is a prerequisite to peacemaking. We confess that we have sinned and fallen short of the glory of God and that we have peace *with* God only by being justified by faith alone in the Lord Jesus Christ (Romans 3:23; 5:1).

The third beatitude bears a special relationship to peacemaking, because there is no way we can pursue peace without submitting to the will of God. Contrary to popular opinion meekness is not weakness, but the special strength that comes from accepting Christ's Lordship over every area of life. The psalmist reminds us that "the meek will inherit the land and enjoy great peace" (Psalm 37:11). The fourth beatitude is also essential for peacemaking. How could we possibly pursue peace without a hunger and thirst for righteousness? Those who "taste and see that the Lord is good" will naturally "turn from evil and do good." They will "seek peace and pursue it" (Psalm 34:8, 14). This was affirmed by James when he wrote, "Peacemakers who sow in peace raise a harvest of righteousness" (James 3:18).

A fifth essential ingredient in the pursuit of peace is mercy. It is natural for those who have received mercy to show mercy and to seek peace. Biblical mercy is not an easy-going tolerance or a look-the-other-way indifference but a demonstration of God's redemptive love. This is why the apostles repeatedly linked mercy and peace together. Paul wrote to the Galatians, "Peace and mercy to all who follow this rule..."(Galatians 6:16) and to Timothy, "Grace, mercy and peace from God the Father and Christ Jesus our Lord" (1 Timothy 1:2; 2 Timothy 1:2). For James to be "peace-loving" was to be "full of mercy" (James 3:17). Peacemaking depended upon the mercy of God. The salutation that the apostle John delivered to earnest believers was anything but conventional, "Grace, mercy and peace from God the Father and from Jesus Christ, the Father's Son, will be with us in truth and love" (2 John 1:3). Finally, the nature of true peacemaking is rooted in the purity of heart that wills one thing. Unless peacemaking is motivated by a self-less, single-minded devotion to God it will not succeed and it will only serve to call attention to human pride and effort. The peace we long for is the Peace of God, for only his peace, "which transcends all understanding, will guard [our] hearts and [our] minds in Christ Jesus" (Philippians 4:7). This is the lasting peace that survives the pain and suffering of this life and outlasts death itself. "You will keep in perfect peace him whose mind is steadfast, because he trusts in you. Trust in the Lord forever, for the Lord, the Lord, is the Rock eternal" (Isaiah 26:3-4). This is the peace that leads to the eschatological peace proclaimed by Isaiah when the nations "will beat their swords into plowshares" (Isaiah 2:4).

These six prerequisites for peacemaking found in the beatitudes go a long way in defining what Jesus meant when he said, "Blessed are the peacemakers, for they will be called the sons of God." If the seventh beatitude is isolated from the rest of the beatitudes and cut off from the biblical meaning of shalom, and separated from its Author, who embodied peacemaking, then it is easy to make peacemaking mean whatever we want it to mean. By disconnecting peacemaking from its roots, what it may gain in popularity it loses in meaning.

World Peace

For many the seventh beatitude expresses the beautiful idealism and moral uplift of a non-conformist Galilean rabbi, a master teacher, who is best remembered in history for inspiring Ghandi-like pacifism and the United Nations' quest for world peace. For those who like to think of the beatitudes as the moral equivalent of Confucian sayings or Benjamin Franklin's aphorisms, the seventh beatitude espouses the highest humanitarian goal. Politicians who would not dare quote the first beatitude love to claim the seventh beatitude. But what is forgotten in their endorsement of peacemaking is that the promise, "for they will be called the sons of God," was given by none other than the Son of God. The meaning of the beatitude does not rest on platitude or principle but on the person of Christ. To strip this beatitude of its theology is to reduce it to propaganda.

Of all the beatitudes this is the one that appears to have universal respect. To acknowledge our need for God and to grieve over our sins sounds woefully pious to the secular person. Meekness, mercy and purity of heart may be sentimentalized as religious rhetoric, but the motto "Blessed are the peacemakers" seems to inspire everyone whether they are religious or secular. Ironically, the words "Shalom" and "Islam" are cognates and mean peace. From the Buddhist monk to the militant "freedom fighter" everyone claims this beatitude as their own because they make it mean what they want it to mean. But what did Jesus mean by the seventh beatitude? Can it be extracted from the other beatitudes and still hold its meaning? Or to put it another way, how does the theology of God's peace relate to the humanitarian quest for peace?

An interesting question to ponder is whether Jesus would have ever received the Nobel Peace Prize. Swedish chemist Alfred Nobel amassed a vast fortune from his invention of dynamite and in his will of 1895 he sought to honor those who had "conferred the greatest benefit on mankind." To that end he endowed five annual awards, for those who had made the most important discoveries in physics, chemistry and medicine, authored "the most outstanding work" of literature and who had "done the most or the best work for fraternity between the nations, for the abolition or reduction of standing armies and for the holding and promotion of peace congresses." Recipients of the Noble Peace Prize include Jimmy Carter, Doctors Without Borders, Yasser Arafat, Yitzhak Rabin, Nelson Mandela, The Dalai Lama, Eli Wiesel, and Desmond Tutu.

The five-member Norwegian panel responsible for choosing the most outstanding "champions of peace" might find some of Jesus' sayings disturbing, such as, "Do not suppose that I have come to bring peace to the earth. I did not come to bring peace, but a sword. For I have come to turn 'a man against his father, a daughter against her mother, a daughter-in-law against her mother-in-law, a man's enemies will be the members of his own household.'" (Matthew 10:34-36).

They would struggle to understand what he meant when he said, "Peace I leave with you; my peace I give you. I do not give to you as the world gives. Do not let your hearts be troubled and do not be afraid" (John 14:27). From a humanistic point of view, Jesus' assurances to his disciples sound egotistical. Who was he to make such outlandish promises, saying "I have told you these things, so that in me you may have peace. In this world you will have trouble. But take heart! I have overcome the world." (John16:33). Who was he to claim that peace resided in a relationship with himself and that he had overcome the world?

Clearly the peacemaking that Jesus pursued went far beyond conflict resolution, troop reductions and political stability. "My peace I give you. I do not give to you as the world gives," claims far more than a blueprint for peace. It means that we need more than a strategy for peace. We need a Savior. The ultimate enmity is not between us, but between us and God. It is doubtful whether the Nobel Peace prize has ever recognized these deeper dimensions of peace. At its root, conflict is not about land or power or race or gender or the have's and the have nots. It is about evil, the God-denying, soul-dividing evil, that separates us from God, from one another, from nature, and from ourselves. Of all people Christians should have no illusions about the depth of depravity in themselves and in the world at large.[90] There is nothing sane or reasonable about evil. Evil is an intractable and obscene absurdity that defies human solution. Such is the power of evil that peacemaking apart from God doesn't have a fighting chance.

Shalom

At this point in our discussion, no one will be surprised to learn that the meaning of Jesus' seventh beatitude is rooted in the Old Testament understanding of peace. If one word captures the essence of salvation and true peace, it is the Hebrew word, *shalom*, which means completeness, soundness, and wholeness. To be at peace is to be whole, to be at rest in our souls and fulfilled in our lives. *Shalom* embraces the fullness of salvation, which means deliverance from "sin and death; guilt and estrangement; ignorance of truth; bondage to habit and vice; fear of demons, of death, of life, of God, of hell; despair of self; alienation from others; pressures of the world; a meaningless life." The meaning of Shalom is exceedingly positive, embracing "peace with God, access to God's favor and presence, hope of regaining the glory intended for humankind, endurance in suffering, steadfast character, an optimistic mind, inner motivations of divine love and power of the Spirit, ongoing experience of the risen Christ and sustaining joy in God."[91]

The peace we long for may include many things, such as health, prosperity, well-being, security, the absence of war, and a release from anxiety. It can be peace of mind, goodwill and harmony with others, personal contentment, and freedom from persecution. But above all else, we long for peace with God, even if we don't identify the longing. As Augustine said in his *Confessions*, "Our hearts are restless until they find their rest in you."[92]

We have to admit that we are incapable of establishing this peace for ourselves. We cannot create Shalom, any more than we can save ourselves. We are poor candidates for peace, our bodies break down, people fail us, terrorists attack, friends betray us, and war breaks out. Where is the peace we long for? The world's strategies for obtaining peace have not been very successful. When the President of the United States confidently declares that America will lead the world to peace, we know we cannot deliver. When "Winston Churchill lay critically ill, he reflected on conditions in the world he had so heroically helped rescue. 'There is no hope,' he sighed. 'There is no hope.' And with the despairing observation, the great leader died but the question survives, 'Is there no hope?' Were Churchill's dying words the epitaph for our age?"[93]

In Isaiah's prophecy of Christ, the four titles culminate in the promise of peace. The wisdom of the Wonderful Counselor, the power of the Mighty God and love of the Everlasting Father leads to the Prince of Peace's enduring peace. The impact of God's work on our behalf, his comforting wisdom, his empowering might, and his everlasting love, provides a lasting peace. Of the four names given to this child who was to be born, the title Prince of Peace seems the most down-to-earth and the most human. It calls attention to the one who will not only establish peace, but embody peace. The Prince of Peace is himself a whole person, "the perfectly integrated, rounded personality, at one with God and humankind, but also a Prince," who administers all these benefits to his people.[94]

"Peace on earth" minus the Prince of Peace is really no peace at all, but an empty slogan. God's Shalom is not imposed, it is bestowed; it is not earned, it is given; it is not achieved, it is received. The peace we long for is not something we can give to ourselves. It is not dependent upon our circumstances, or our health or on those around us. God's peace is not achieved through military might or romantic love or material success. It is achieved by the Prince of Peace, whose task it was "to reconcile to himself all things, whether things on earth or things in heaven, by making peace through his blood, shed on the cross" (Colossians 1:20). If you do not know the Prince of Peace you can receive him today. You can bow before him and ask him to rule and reign in your life.

Shalom is the gift of God that is based on a personal relationship with Jesus Christ, who paid the price for our peace. Isaiah's prophecy moves us from the exalted titles to the humble sacrifice, from the manger to the Cross: "Surely he took up our infirmities and carried our sorrows, yet we considered him stricken by God, smitten by him, and afflicted.

But he was pierced for our transgressions, he was crushed for our iniquities; the punishment that brought us peace was upon him, and by his wounds we are healed" (Isaiah 53:4-5). Because of Christ's sacrifice, the apostle Paul was able to write, "Therefore, since we have been justified through faith, we have peace with God through our Lord Jesus Christ..." (Romans 5:1). *The Gift we celebrate receiving at Christmas was not wrapped, it was crucified, it was not under the tree, it was nailed to the tree; and it was not opened on Christmas day, it was opened on Easter morning.* Christmas declares that Shalom and Salvation are dependent upon the Savior. "Today...a Savior has been born to you; he is Christ the Lord." Apart from the Prince of Peace there is no salvation and there is no shalom. "Glory to God in the highest, and on earth peace to all on whom his favor rests." Apart from God's Glory and without God's Grace there is no Peace.

Simeon foresaw the price of peace when he held the baby Jesus in his arms and said to Mary, "This child is destined to cause the falling and rising of many in Israel, and to be a sign that will be spoken against, so that the thoughts of many hearts will be revealed. And a sword will pierce your own soul too" (Luke 2:34-35). Jesus knew that the gift of peace would be scorned by many. This is why he said, "Do not suppose that I have come to bring peace to the earth. I did not come to bring peace, but a sword" (Matthew 10:34), prompting Oswald Chambers to write, "Jesus Christ came to send a sword through every kind of peace that is not based on a personal relationship with Himself."[95] John Calvin declared, "Peace with God is contrasted with every form of intoxicated security in the flesh."

Jesus was under no illusion that the world would find his peace acceptable. His followers can expect to experience trials and tribulation in the world, but ultimately the peace of Christ will prevail. "I have told you these things," Jesus said, "so that in me you may have peace. In this world you will have trouble. But take heart! I have overcome the world." (John 16:33).

Cheap Peace

"Shalom" was a key word in the prophet Jeremiah's day as well, but it was reduced to empty rhetoric in the mouths of leaders who used the word but despised its true meaning. Jeremiah voiced the Lord's perspective on these clever manipulators when he said, "They dress the wound of my people as though it were not serious. 'Peace, peace' they say, when there is no peace" (Jeremiah 6:14, see 8:11). Although the people deserved judgment for their evil ways, their leaders persisted in promising them peace. Jeremiah complained to God, "Ah, Sovereign LORD, the prophets keep telling them, 'You will not see the sword or suffer famine. Indeed, I will give you lasting peace in this place'" (Jeremiah 14:13).

In Jeremiah's day the false prophets defined peace "merely as the absence of turmoil and social conflict, and not as the triumph of divine righteousness among people."[96] They refused to distinguish between belief and unbelief, fidelity and idolatry, sexual purity and sexual immorality. And they failed to discern the difference between conforming to the spirit of the age and submitting to the Word of the Lord. Then as now, religious leaders use peacemaking as an excuse for appeasement. They advocate a "live-and-let-live" philosophy of life that tolerates evil and compromises the truth.

Jeremiah was led by the Lord to deliver an either/or message that was reminiscent of the challenge Moses gave to the Israelites (Deuteronomy 30:15,19): "This is what the Lord says: 'See, I am setting before you the way of life and the way of death'" (Deuteronomy 21:8). But the leadership felt no compulsion to choose. They wanted it both ways. They wanted to copy the ways of the world, condone pagan practices, conform to the spirit of the times but also maintain affiliation with their religious heritage. Jeremiah challenged their both/and thinking with simple dualisms, stark alternatives, red and green logic, black and white choices. He contended that obedience was clear cut and faithfulness unambiguous. There was no in-between gray areas that allowed Judah's leaders to please Yahweh and also appease Baal, or exploit the poor and rescue the poor. They had to choose one or the other. They had simple options. The choice was theirs.

Like the "shepherds" in Jeremiah's day there are religious leaders today who mock what they call the "simplistic bifurcation" that pits "us" against "them" in matters related to biblical faith and practice. I imagine that they would condemn Jeremiah for his "destructive binary oppositions" and his "troublesome polarization." They speak of "inclusivity" and "wholeness" and assure us that radically divergent theological perspectives belong together. They intentionally confuse racial and ethnic diversity with radical pluralism. Their watchword is "shalom" but they advocate peace at any price. Like the prophets in Micah's day they promise peace at bargain basement prices, a peace without repentance and forgiveness (Micah 3:5). What Dietrich Bonhoeffer said of cheap grace applies to cheap peace: "Cheap *peace* is *peace* without discipleship, *peace* without the cross, *peace* without Jesus Christ, living and incarnate."[97]

No one emphasized the either/or alternative more than Jesus. We might prefer an indecisive "maybe," or a kind of middle-of-the-road, *whatever* belief system, but Jesus did not give us that option. What we get in Jesus' Sermon on the Mount is a series of either/or alternatives: two ways (broad and narrow), two teachers (false and true), two pleas (words and deeds) and finally two foundations (sand and rock). Jesus ends his message with a parable about two kinds of builders: one who builds on the rock and one who builds on the sand. Jesus established a clear line and a sharp contrast between wisdom and foolishness, between cheap peace and costly peace. We are compelled by the Lord to do the same thing.

Costly Peace

Make no mistake, peacemaking involves a holy war, but not in the sense of a Moslem "jihad" that seeks to destroy the enemy and impose the rule of Allah. Nor is it a holy war in the tradition of the conquistadors and the crusaders who sought to impose a Christ-less Christianity. It is a holy war in the tradition of Jesus who made peace through his blood shed on the cross (Colossians 1:20). This is why the apostle Paul said, "Put on the full armor of God so that you can take your stand against the devil's schemes. For our struggle is not against flesh and blood, but against the rulers, against the authorities, against the powers of this dark world and against the spiritual forces of evil in the heavenly realms"(Ephesians 6:11-12).

"The gospel of Jesus Christ is more political than anyone imagines, but in a way that no one guesses."[98] When we pray, "Your kingdom come, your will be done on earth as it is in heaven," we are not campaigning for God to support our national interests. We are not wrapping the cross in our political agenda or baptizing family values or empowering "the moral majority". To do this would be to confuse the Kingdom of God with our country. What we are praying is that God will make us instruments of *his peace*, not the peace of the world, but the gospel of peace that brings everyone and everything under the rule of God. The advance of the gospel was meant to inspire hope, not fear. The prophet Isaiah described the compassionate advance of the gospel, "How beautiful on the mountains are the feet of those who bring good news, who proclaim peace, who bring good tidings, who proclaim salvation, who say to Zion, 'Your God reigns!'" (Isaiah 52:7).

Jesus ended the seventh beatitude with a promise, "Blessed are the peacemakers for they will be called the children of God." Peacemaking is the sign of our family identity. Like a son takes after his father so we are to take after

God our Father. Jesus gave the same promise when he said, "Love your enemies and pray for those who persecute you, that you may be sons of your Father in heaven." He even went so far as to say, "Be perfect as your heavenly Father is perfect" (Matthew 5:44, 48). In the seventh beatitude it becomes clear that what Jesus said about his relationship with the Father is also true for us. You recall that Jesus said, "I tell you the truth, the Son can do nothing by himself; he can do only what he sees his Father doing, because whatever the Father does the Son also does. For the Father loves the Son and shows him all he does" (John 5:19-20). The God of Peace (Hebrews 13:20) took the initiative and became a man, "he humbled himself and became obedient to death—even death on a cross!" (Philippians 2:8). "If God stood upon His rights and dignity, upon His Person, every one of us, and the whole of humankind, would be consigned to hell and absolute perdition. It is because God is a 'God of peace' that he sent His Son, and thus provided a way of salvation for us. To be a peacemaker is to be like God, and like the Son of God."[99]

Since God has taken the initiative to bring about our reconciliation, we who have been reconciled in Christ can take the initiative and humble ourselves. We are freed up to pursue peace because "from now on we regard no one from a worldly point of view" (2 Corinthians 5:16). We have not only been reconciled to God in Christ but we have been given the ministry of reconciliation. The apostle Paul's exhortations do not fall on deaf ears, when he says, "If it is possible, as far as it depends on you, live at peace with everyone," and "Do not be overcome by evil, but overcome evil with good" (Romans 12:18). Because of the grace of Christ it is possible to "Let the peace of Christ rule in [our] hearts, since as members of one body [we] were called to peace. And be thankful" (Colossians 3:15).

"May the God of peace, who through the blood of the eternal covenant brought back from the dead our Lord Jesus, that great Shepherd of the sheep, equip you with everything good for doing his will, and may he work in us what is pleasing to him, through Jesus Christ, to whom be glory for ever and ever. Amen."

Hebrews 13:20-21

"The Lord bless you and keep you; the Lord make his face shine upon you and be gracious to you; the Lord turn his face toward you and give you peace."

Numbers 6:24-26

8

Suffering Persecution

"Blessed are those who are persecuted because of righteousness, for theirs is the kingdom of heaven."

Matthew 5:10

The description of the disciple of Jesus is not complete without this eighth beatitude. It follows naturally from the seven previous beatitudes. It is consistent with the New Testament description of the church and it is especially relevant to the world-wide Body of Christ. Believers in India, Pakistan, China, Iran, Egypt, North Korea, Myanmar (Burma), Laos, and Sudan are being pressured, imprisoned and murdered because they are Christians. We read the apostle Paul's letter from a Roman prison in the safety and security of our homes, in a land that is blessed with religious freedom and tolerance, but many of our brothers and sisters in Christ hear Paul's words differently. Paul wrote, "I consider everything a loss compared to the surpassing greatness of knowing Christ Jesus my Lord, for whose sake I have lost all things. I consider them rubbish that I may gain Christ.... I want to know Christ and the power of his resurrection and the fellowship of sharing in his sufferings, becoming like him in his death...." (Philippians 3:8,10).

The Fellowship of His Suffering

Nigerian Nvou Dauda knows the fellowship of Christ's sufferings. Militant Muslims raided her village in Nigeria's Plateau State on December 8, 2002. She was shot in the hand, stomach and leg, because she would not convert to Islam. Her attackers torched her home after dousing it with gasoline. Her

2-year-old son died in the deadly inferno. Nvou was seven months pregnant at the time of the attack and her unborn baby was killed by the gunshot that pierced her stomach. Nvou is one of more than 450 persecuted Nigerian Christians who have received surgery and medical treatment from doctors with *Voice of the Martyrs* (a mission organization that serves the persecuted church – www.persecution.com). "I've handed everything over to God," explained Nvou, "and I pray He will take care of me. I will continue to work for God; and even if I am killed, it will mean I was killed in the name of the Lord."

Sadly her story is not unique. Millions of believers face political persecution because their faith in Christ offends government ideology. They agree with the apostle Peter when he said to the officials, "Judge for yourselves whether it is right in God's sight to obey you rather than God. For we cannot help speaking about what we have seen and heard" (Acts 4:19-20). One-fourth of the world's population still lives under communist rule. House church pastors in China are routinely imprisoned for what they preach. Pastor Li Dexian has been arrested numerous times for teaching on Christ's return, a subject banned in the official government church.

Laotian Communist leaders implemented a new program called the "New Mechanism" which forces Christians to convert to Buddhism or animism or be forcibly removed from their village. Tens of thousands of North Koreans are imprisoned, and officials reportedly consider the worst of these prisoners to be the Christians.

Millions of other believers endure religious repression and terrorism. After years of the Taliban's brutal repression of the church, there is a new openness to the gospel in Afghanistan. Algerian Christians have had to face a reign of terror from the Islamic Salvation Front. Militant Muslims have marched through towns slitting the throats of those who reject Islamic fundamentalism. Christians are second class citizens and routinely discriminated against in Bangladesh, Cyprus, Egypt, Turkey, and Syria. In many countries evangelism is against the law. In Pakistan and Nigeria, Christians are subject to mob violence, and in southern Sudan they continue to be victims of genocide. "A time is coming," Jesus warned, "when anyone who kills you will think he is offering a service to God" (John 16:2).

Many in the Body of Christ hear the words of Jesus with a sense of immediacy and intensity that those of us in the American church do not feel or understand. "If the world hates you, keep in mind that it hated me first.... Remember the words I spoke to you: 'No servant is greater than his master.' If they persecuted me, they will persecute you also" (John 15:20). Dietrich Bonhoeffer wrote, "Suffering is the badge of true discipleship," but many Christians seem to think that success is the sign of God's blessing.[100]

Ethicist Paul Marshall was one of the first to tell the untold story of persecution against Christians in the modern world in his book *Their Blood Cries Out*. He documents the world-wide plague of religious persecution and calls for an international lament. He describes the advancing Jihad and Communism's continuing grip. He analyzes American Christianity's agenda of "peace at any price." Marshall contends that we have shut out the world-wide body of Christ and focused on inner peace and outward success. Instead of being persecuted, Christians are often preoccupied with simple formulas for spiritual success, self-help strategies, entertaining worship, and our emotional well-being. Our brothers and sisters in Christ are in the throes of the eighth beatitude and we are debating worship styles. Some believers risk their livelihood and their lives to worship together, but we excuse our absence from worship because of the pressures of our work week.[101]

Jesus did not promise the church peace and prosperity; he promised peace in the midst of persecution and suffering.

In fact he said, "Woe to you when all people speak well of you, for that is how their fathers treated the false prophets" (Luke 6:26). "Since all the beatitudes describe what every Christian disciple is intended to be," writes John Stott, "we conclude that the condition of being despised and rejected, slandered and persecuted, is as much a normal mark of Christian discipleship as being pure in heart or merciful."[102] "The fellowship of the beatitudes is the fellowship of the Crucified. With him it has lost all, and with him it has found all." The apostle Paul put it simply when he said, "...Everyone who wants to live a godly life in Christ Jesus will be persecuted" (2 Timothy 3:12).

Christians in the West tend to distance themselves from the persecuted Body of Christ or they end up fighting battles that Jesus never would have fought. Many seem to forget that Jesus said to Pilate, "My kingdom is not of this world. If it were, my servants would fight to prevent my arrest by the Jews. But now my kingdom is from another place" (John 18:36). On the steps of the Alabama State Court House, well-meaning Christians felt persecuted because the Federal Court decided that the monument to the Ten Commandments must be removed. I was struck by the raw anger of some of the Christians who sought to defy the court order removing the monument. Would they prefer that the court sanction the monument on the basis of ceremonial deism? Are they willing to concede that the God referred to in the first commandment is a generic deity respected by religious people in order to keep their monument in the public square? Or is this the one, true and living God who is personally and uniquely revealed in the Incarnate One, Jesus Christ?

Many Christians cherish our national motto, "In God We Trust" and the phrase "one nation under God" in our Pledge of Allegiance, but Supreme Court Justice O'Connor argues that these phrases are not to be "understood as conveying government approval of particular religious beliefs" because they express "an essentially secular meaning." According to Justice Brennan, these phrases have become dead platitudes. They "have lost through rote repetition any significant content."[104]

The Gospel of Jesus Christ was never meant to be imposed on people. The doctrines of religious freedom and tolerance are based on the Gospel of Grace. The followers of Jesus must not intimidate, indoctrinate or impose the truth of God on others. I doubt that those who want the monument to stand in the court house want a statue of Buddha placed next to it. What many American Christians fail to understand is the difference between Christianizing America and living for Christ in America. The former agenda requires worldly power; the latter agenda involves taking up a cross and following Jesus.

Vinay Samuel, Director of the International Fellowship of Evangelical Mission Theologians, defines religious fanatics as those who "feel called to take the world by its neck and conform it to their vision of what the world should be like. To do that, they will sacrifice everything, including themselves."[105] An extreme example of a religious fanatic is former Presbyterian minister Paul Hill who murdered a doctor and his bodyguard in 1994 because the doctor performed abortions. Right up to his execution Hill remained defiant and unrepentant. He said, "I believe the state, by executing me, will be making me a martyr."[106] Not unlike the Palestinian suicide bombers, Paul Hill died in vain. The religious fanatic refuses to see the difference between murder and martyrdom—between committing a hate crime and seeking social justice—because in the name of righteousness he rejects Christ's righteousness. Instead of submitting to the will of God, he asserts his own will. His cause is absolute and he is willing to sacrifice all things, including himself and the will of God.

The apostle Peter's spiritual direction and encouragement to the persecuted church offers an important perspective on the eighth beatitude. He challenged and comforted them at the same time, when he said, "Live such good lives among the pagans that, though they accuse you of doing wrong, they may see your good deeds and glorify God on the day he visits us.... Live as free men and women, but do not use your freedom as a cover-up for evil; live as servants of God.... Live in harmony with one another; be sympathetic, love as brothers, be compassionate and humble. Do not repay evil with evil or insult with insult, but with blessing, because to this you were called so that you may inherit a blessing" (1 Peter 2:12, 16; 3:8-9).

It is important for the followers of Christ everywhere, but especially in the West, to realize that the eighth beatitude is not an anti-climax but a climax to all the beatitudes. It is not the optional beatitude, added as an afterthought, but the essential beatitude that builds on all the rest. The previous beatitudes help the believer understand what it means to be persecuted because of righteousness. They instruct us in the legitimate causes of persecution — what it means to be insulted, persecuted, and slandered for Christ's sake. Together, they not only give us a portrait of the believer but the criteria for biblical resistance. In other words, if the first seven beatitudes describe your life, you can be sure you'll experience the eighth.

The Seven-fold Criteria for Biblical Resistance

Believers who live for Christ in countries hostile to faith in Christ understand their dependence upon the Lord in ways many Western believers find difficult to comprehend. They understand what it is to be "poor in spirit" and to turn to God out of desperate need. Understandably, it seems much easier for them to cherish the promise of the Kingdom of God than it does for us who live in an affluent, self-indulgent, pleasure-seeking culture. A Pakistani believer by the name of Raheem understands this beatitude. His church showed the JESUS film for three months on the streets of Karachi. Then, Islamic radicals spread the rumor that someone from the church had reportedly burned a Koran, an offense punishable by death under Pakistan's Law 295. Seventy Christians were arrested, and militant Muslims called for revenge by burning homes owned by Christians and beating Christian men and raping Christian woman. Raheem was arrested, imprisoned, and beaten 100 times on the bottom of his feet. When he was eventually released he explained that the ordeal had neither embittered nor intimidated him, but in fact had strengthened his faith and commitment to Christ. Raheem can identify with the apostle Paul when he wrote, "When we are cursed, we bless; when we are persecuted, we endure it; when we are slandered, we answer kindly. Up to this moment we have become the scum of the earth, the refuse of the world" (1 Corinthians 4:12-13).

Believers who have been persecuted for Christ's sake understand the depths of depravity and what it means to mourn and grieve over sin. They have been pushed beyond hate to love. John Perkins, in his book *A Quiet Revolution*, describes the night he was brutally beaten by the police in Brandon, Mississippi. He had participated in a nonviolent civil rights march earlier in the day and had been arrested. He writes:

> *"During the night in the jail at Brandon, God began something new in my life. In the midst of the crowded noisy jailhouse, between the stomping and the black-jacking that we received; between the moments when one of the patrolmen put his pistol to my head and pulled the trigger — 'click' — and when another later took a fork and bent the two middle prongs down and pushed the other two up my nose until blood came out — between the reality and the insanity, between the consciousness and the unconsciousness that sweep across my dizzy mind, between my terror and my unwillingness to break down, between my pain and my fear, in those little snatches of thought when in some miraculous way I could at once be the spectacle and the spectator, God pushed me past hatred. Just for a little while, moments at a time.*

How could I hate when there was so much to pity? How could I hate people I suddenly did not recognize, who had somehow moved past the outer limits of what it means to be human...? But I don't think it was just the pity I had or the deep sickness I saw alone that pushed me past hate. It was also the fact that I was broken.... The Brandon experience just might have been a way of God bringing me to the place where he could expand his love in me and extend my calling to white people as well as black people.... And I believe that it was in my own broken state that the depth of the sickness in those men struck home to me, and the fact that I was like them — totally depraved. I had evidence before me and in myself that every human being is bad — depraved. There's something built into all of us that makes us want to be superior. If the black man had the advantage, he'd be just as bad. So I can't hate the white man. It's a spiritual problem — black or white, we all need to be born again...

The failure, the frustration, the powerlessness of my situation as a black person in the South pressed me. What it was squeezing out of me was more and more bitterness. Like a lemon — so fresh and sweet looking on the outside but hiding such a sour taste. And the bitterness just made the frustration worse.

I saw how bitterness could destroy me. The Spirit of God had a hold of me and wouldn't let me sidestep his justice. And his justice said that I was just as sinful as those who beat me. But I knew that God's justice is seasoned with forgiveness. Forgiveness is what makes his justice redemptive. Forgiveness! That was the key. And somehow, God's forgiveness for me was tied up in my forgiveness of those who hurt me.

'For if you forgive men when they sin against you, your heavenly Father will also forgive you. But if you do not forgive men their sins, your Father will not forgive your sins' (Matthew 6:14-15).

We were right. . . . But now God was saying, 'Being right is not enough. You must also be forgiving.' Reconciliation is so difficult because the damage is so deep."[107]

Because of the grace of Christ, John Perkins was pushed beyond hate to love. Instead of responding to persecution with animosity and hate, he learned the power of forgiveness and love. One of the blessings of being able to mourn for our sins and receive the forgiveness of Christ is the transformation of our anger. In Christ we have the grace-filled capacity to love instead of hate.

Believers who learn to submit to God's will discover that meekness is not weakness, but it often brings on persecution. Early in my pastoral ministry at our church in San Diego, I was branded by some as legalistic, pharisaical, and homophobic. The leadership of the church had voted to submit to the authority of the Bible on the hotly debated issue of homosexuality. They agreed that "participation in, and/or endorsement of, deviant sexual behavior such as pre-marital sex, adultery and same gender sex" was grounds for termination of employment. Within the week the organist, who was gay, resigned. He expressed how "stunned, shocked, and deeply hurt" he was. Even though the church had struggled with this issue for months, he claimed he never would have accepted a position in a church where his sexuality would have been a problem. He clearly saw himself as suffering for the sake of the gospel and persecuted by narrow-minded, pharisaical literalists.

The tension in our church was so real, so palpable, that I could feel the weight of it against my chest. On the Sunday after this decision was made, when I stood up to preach a number of choir members stood up and walked out. One person marched up to me after the service and, extending her hand, said, 'I've always wanted to shake the hand of a bigot!" A retired Presbyterian pastor, seething with anger, wagged his finger in my face, and accused me of splitting the church. Another member announced, "After today, I am ashamed to be called a Presbyterian. And YOU call yourself a pastor?!" Others told me that I was responsible for destroying the church and that in no time we would be "closing the doors of the church." A leading pastor in the Presbytery said to me, "It doesn't take any skill to come into a church and blow it up. Anyone can do that." I received mail that accused me of "Nazi type tactics" and a package with nothing in it but a picture of a gun with a finger on the trigger.

There was, of course, nothing heroic about the stand we took, and I derived no pleasure from antagonizing people. I am not a crusader and I did not want my ministry defined by a single moral issue. I am simply a disciple of the Lord Jesus Christ who seeks to live under the authority of God's Word. It was an act of obedience, not defiance, a simple case of meekness, based on a desire to be true to the Word of Truth. I felt like a person under orders, whose commanding officer had given a directive. My prayer was that we would hold to biblical conviction with biblical compassion, and that we would speak the truth in love.

The fourth beatitude is important for defining the true nature of persecution. Believers who hunger and thirst after righteousness will suffer persecution for Christ's sake. Dietrich Bonhoeffer observed, "It is important that Jesus gives his blessing, not merely to suffering incurred directly for the confession of his name, but to suffering in any just cause."[108] Others however, have contended that unless persecution is directed against preaching or evangelizing, it is not persecution for Christ's sake. Martyn Lloyd-Jones argues for this "vital distinction" when he writes:

> *"We must also realize that it does not mean suffering persecution for religio-political reasons. Now it is the simple truth to say that there were Christian people in Nazi Germany who were not only ready to practice and live the Christian faith but who preached it in the open air and yet were not molested. But we know of certain others who were put into prisons and concentration camps, and*

we should be careful to see why this happened to them. And I think if you draw that distinction you will find it was generally political. I need not point out that I am not attempting to excuse Hitlerism; but I am trying to remind every Christian person of this vital distinction. If you and I begin to mix our religion and politics, then we must not be surprised if we receive persecution. But I suggest that it will not of necessity be persecution for righteousness' sake. This is something very distinct and particular, and one of the greatest dangers confronting us is that of not discriminating between these two things. There are Christian people in China and on the Continent at the present time to whom this is the most acute problem of all. Are they standing for righteousness' sake, or for a cause?...If you choose to suffer politically, go on and do so. But do not have a grudge against God if you find that this Beatitude, this promise, is not verified in your life. The Beatitude and the promise refer specifically to suffering for righteousness' sake. May God give us grace and wisdom and understanding to discriminate between our political prejudices and our spiritual principles."[109]*

With all due respect to the ministry of Martyn Lloyd-Jones, his position on persecution is regrettable and unbiblical. Hitler sought to use the church to further his policies and his doctrines. Under the pretext of renewal and revitalization he infused the church with German nationalism. In the early years the Nazis "did not persecute the Church; they sought to pervert it. Hitler wished to keep the Church intact as a subservient instrument, furthering this policy and proclaiming his doctrines."[110] Hitler exchanged "a hero Jesus" for what he despised as "the demoralizing 'Suffering Servant.'" He substituted the German race for the Body of Christ. Nazi propaganda insisted that as Jesus rescued people from sin and hell, so Hitler rescued the German people from destruction. "Jesus built for heaven; Hitler, for the German earth."[111] If someone had shouted at a Nazi political rally, "Jesus is the Savior!" no one would have paid him any attention, because Nazism and the "German People's Church" were one. But if someone had said "Jesus is my Fuhrer," he would have been thrown into prison. Hitler used the church to promote his anti-Jewish, racist, personality cult and the German Church let him get away with it because it conveniently compartmentalized their faith. Hitler ruled in the political realm and Jesus in the spiritual realm.

The Confessing Church movement under the leadership of Karl Barth, Martin Niemoller, Dietrich Bonhoeffer and others risked their lives to oppose Hitler. They issued the Barmen Declaration in 1934 which set forth with clarity the Faith of the Confessing Church and boldly rejected the false teaching that subverted the Lordship of Jesus Christ by a false allegiance to political ideology and special leaders (Fuhrer). "We repudiate the false teaching that there are areas of our life in which we belong not to Jesus Christ but another lord, areas in which we do not need justification and sanctification through him.... We repudiate the false teaching that the State can and should expand beyond its special responsibility to become the single and total order of human life, and also thereby fulfill the commission of the Church."[112] The Barmen Declaration became the charter of the resistance, and those who refused to deny it, "lost their livelihood, accepted imprisonment, were exiled, and some of them died."[113] The German Confessing Church like the house church movement in China refused to be a subservient instrument of the State and because of their faithfulness to Christ they were persecuted for righteousness' sake.

The fifth beatitude further qualifies the quality of life that brings about persecution. Showing mercy and doing good in the name of Christ "should silence the ignorant talk of foolish people" but sometimes it leads to "the pain of unjust suffering" (1 Peter 2:15, 19). We would expect that those who show mercy would receive mercy, not only from the Lord but from the world, but that is often not the case. The ministry of mercy is often met with hostility. Muslim fanatics in Pakistan have been burning Christian hospitals that have cared for the poor for more than 100 years. Nurses have been killed and doctors intimidated. Medical missionaries Steve and Sue Befus ministered to thousands of Liberians for twenty years but rebels ransacked their hospital three times and treated them like enemies. Unarmed and unprotected, they were in today's parlance "soft targets," but they continued to show mercy in spite of the persecution.

The sixth beatitude refines the nature of biblical resistance by removing the self-serving ego and by refusing to regard anyone from "a worldly point of view" (2 Corinthians 5:16). We no longer see people as we once did, out of our prejudices and biases, but as men and women for whom Christ died. "If your enemy is hungry, feed him; if he is thirsty, give him something to drink. In doing this, you will heap burning coals on his head" (Romans 12:20). The purity of heart that wills one thing draws persecution for all the right reasons. Painful trials, insults and slander come not because we are trying to make a name for ourselves, but "because of the name of Christ" (1 Peter 4:14).

Tim Stafford reports that faithful and effective evangelists in Sri Lanka are distancing themselves from any kind of incentive or inducement that would falsify conversions or lead to "unethical conversions." They want the pure power of the Gospel to change lives rather than the excitement of special events and the material support that often comes from foreign mission agencies. "The Evangelical Alliance of Sri Lanka has issued guidelines for church planting. They say evangelism should avoid the visible presence of foreigners, eschew disrespectful comments about other religions, and avoid publicizing special events. Church leaders told me that they encourage evangelists not to use loudspeakers, not to put up signs, and not to let services spill outdoors. The best evangelists seem to be families who can sustain themselves through a trade or other business; the best strategy seems to be the house church."[114] Christians in Sri Lanka are a small minority between two rival ethnic factions made up of the Buddhist Sinhalese people and the Hindu Tamils. In so far as it depends on them, faithful believers want to be persecuted for the right thing. They don't want to draw fire because of Western funding, aggressive tactics, material incentives, and manipulation. If they are persecuted they want it to be because of genuine conversions, not "unethical conversions."

The seventh criteria of biblical resistance and the capstone qualification for being persecuted for righteousness' sake is peacemaking. The cause for persecution is never because the disciple of Christ poses a worldly threat. The world should never have to fear a Christian. Those who persecute, insult, threaten, slander, swindle, and murder Christians are never in danger of receiving the same treatment they themselves perpetrate and perpetuate. That is not to say that Christians cannot defend others and themselves from violence, slander, deception and terrorism. But it is to say that the disciple of the Lord Jesus Christ does not fight the way the world does. "For though we live in the world, we do not wage war as the world does. The weapons we fight with are not the weapons of the world" (2 Corinthians 10:4). Christians should be fearless, not fearsome. They should be faithful, not frightful. Since they do not have to fear what the world fears (1 Peter 3:14) they do not have to act the way the world acts.

One month after the September 11, 2001 terrorist attack, *Christianity Today* editor Mark Galli summarized a practical response to religious terrorism. He wrote:

> *"The struggle must be waged on a variety of fronts: Christians praying always and everywhere; missionaries and local believers hazarding their lives in sharing the gospel in the most religiously repressive settings; relief agencies and local congregations refusing to discriminate in distributing aid to the needy; Christian diplomats employing all the wiles of their craft; and, yes, Christian fighter pilots, navy personnel, and infantry insisting,*

*when other options are exhausted and military force is
called for, that liberty be respected and justice done."*[115]

If believers follow this seven-fold criteria for biblical
resistance they can be assured that the persecution they
experience is for Christ's sake. Moreover they can be assured
that they are following the example of the Lord Jesus, because
no one met this criteria better than the Crucified and Risen
Lord. "If you suffer for doing good and you endure it, this is
commendable before God," wrote the apostle Peter. "To this
you were called, because Christ suffered for you, leaving you
an example, that you should follow in his steps" (1 Peter 2:20-21).

The Path to the Cross

It is scandalous that one who healed the sick, loved the outcast,
and transformed the sinner should die a hideously cruel death
by Roman crucifixion. What kind of world do we live in that
sentences holy and compassionate men and women to die?
Jesus exposes the fact that the political and religious authorities
are not always on the side of righteousness. Greed, pride, and
hate often control the power brokers of society. Jesus became
a victim for the sake of righteousness. It was impossible for
anyone living in the first century to gloss over the practical
social consequences of following Jesus. The Cross made sure of
that. Early Christians knew that their lives were marked by the
Cross, but today many contemporary, conservative Christians
give the impression that a decision for Jesus simply involves
submitting mentally to the idea that Jesus died for their sins.

On the other hand, those who wish to emphasize the
political side of Jesus' death tend to ignore the circumstantial
evidence of the Gospels. Jesus' message clearly had political
impact, yet he was completely different from the Zealots and
decidedly less dangerous. He resisted violence (Luke 9:54-55;
John 18:10-11), rejected popular support (John 2:24; 6:15), and flatly

denied that his kingdom was of the world (John 18:36). He neither defended the status quo nor encouraged revolution. He refused to be tricked into nationalism. He insisted on God's authority over all of life, without making a secular-spiritual dichotomy (Mark 12:17; John 19:11). He narrowed his loyal supporters down to a small band of men and women but right up to the end remained accessible to the public through his daily teaching (Mark 14:48-49). The meaning of his life simply cannot be exhausted politically. Although his death has tremendous political significance, he lived and died for something far more significant than a political cause. This truth is part of the confusion and the tragedy of the Cross. From a political point of view, Jesus did not have to die. It is true that the Jewish Sanhedrin feared for their social privilege and political influence, but this fear alone was not sufficient to account for his death (John 11:48).

To contend that Jesus' strategy of nonviolence and his condemnation of those who wielded the sword resulted in the death penalty goes beyond the evidence. It is difficult to support the conclusion that Jesus was a greater political threat than Barabbas. John Yoder's observation seems exaggerated: "His alternative was so relevant, so much a threat, that Pilate could afford to free, in exchange for Jesus, the ordinary Guevara type insurrectionist Barabbas."[116]

The Gospels do not develop the political impact of Jesus sufficiently to lead logically and inevitably to the Cross. This inability to explain Jesus' death simply in political terms is part of the frustration and despair of the Cross. Pilate did not have to kill Jesus. Nowhere is it suggested that he considered Jesus a greater threat to Roman rule than Barabbas. If anything, he probably released Barabbas and sentenced Jesus only to pacify the Jews. His judgment was not decided because he feared the political impact of Jesus' civil disobedience. In all likelihood, much of what Jesus said and did escaped Pilate's notice. The death of Jesus was a relatively small matter for Pilate. Politically speaking, Jesus could have walked away a free man instead of being nailed to the cross.

Part of the scandal of the Cross is that God's purposes are accomplished and his Word is fulfilled in the midst of political ambiguity and seemingly accidental circumstances. I remember being troubled as a 13-year-old by the death of Dr. Paul Carlson, a medical missionary in the Republic of Congo. Carlson had been falsely accused by the rebel Simbas of being a major in the American military, a mercenary, instead of a missionary doctor. On November 24, as Belgium paratroopers were landing in Stanleyville, Carlson along with a number of other hostages were led by their Simba guards out into the middle of the street while guns were firing all around the area. In the mad confusion some of the hostages were hit. Some ran for the nearest protection. A small group ran to the shelter of a house and clambered over the porch wall. One of the hostages leaped over the wall and reached back. He had his fingers on Paul's sweater when a young Simba came around the corner and fired off five shots, instantly killing Paul Carlson. A second or two later and he would have been on the other side of the wall. His body was graphically shown throughout the world on the glossy pages of *Life* magazine.

At the time, he seemed to me more a victim of tragic circumstances than an ambassador for Christ who gave his life for the gospel. Since then, I have come to see that the Christian's cross, like Jesus' cross, must be interpreted on two levels. On the one level, confusion and ambiguity surround the meaning and interpretation of our lives. From this perspective, Dr. Carlson's death was nothing more than meaningless circumstances leading to a tragedy that might easily have been averted. But what may appear to be a tragic, accidental moment is in fact an orchestrated movement in the sovereign plan of God. In so many ways, Paul Carlson died like his Lord.

On the one hand, Jesus appears as the victim of circumstances—a friend betrays him, popular sentiment turns against him, a ruler concerned only with political expediency hears his case, and his disciples abandon him. But on the other hand, Jesus dies (in accord with Old Testament prophecy) as the lamb who was slain from the foundation of the world (Luke 24:25-27; 1 Peter 1:20; Revelation 13:8). There is an inevitability about his death that lies outside historical circumstances and human arrangements. It is impossible to adequately understand the suffering and death of Jesus apart from God's interpretation of the event. God infuses the Cross with meaning from three primary sources: the history of God's revelation to Israel, Jesus' self-disclosure, and the apostolic witness. There is a tremendous redemptive purpose arising out of the muddle of historical circumstances. This glorious purpose is not the product of human imagination and wishful thinking. It is the fulfillment of God's eternal plan of redemption. The real scandal of the Cross lies in the fact that God in Christ, the Savior of the world, was crucified.

Nor did Paul Carlson die as an isolated martyr. His wife, Lois, and their two children, Wayne and Lynette, have continued to pay the price of persecution for righteousness' sake. You can imagine my surprise when I learned that Paul Carlson's daughter Lyn attended our church. I had spoken to Lyn from time to time and thanked her for helping out in our Ladle ministry (our humanitarian and evangelistic outreach to the poor and homeless), but I never connected her last name to her father. Then one day, I was chatting with the director of our Ladle ministry Allen Randall in his office. I noticed on his desk the 1964 *Life* magazine issue with the picture of Paul Carlson on the cover. I began to explain to Allen how I had struggled with Paul Carlson's death when I was a young teenager. "Well, did you know that Lyn is his daughter?" Allen asked. Since then, Lyn and I have talked about her father and the struggles she has gone through because of his death. It has made me wonder who suffered more, her father who was cut down in an instant or Lyn who has lived for years in the confusion and absence of her father. Through our conversations I have a deeper sense of how suffering for Christ can be passed down from generation to generation. Paul Carlson lost his life and gained heaven, but Lyn lost her father and experienced a difficult life. Martyrdom comes in different forms. Lyn likened her own struggle to Isaac, Abraham's son, who was forced to deal with his father's actions when he laid him on the altar and prepared to sacrifice him. Life did not turn out the way Lyn expected, but through it all, Lyn has lived for Christ in such a way that her father would be proud of her even as her heavenly Father is pleased with her. With God's help she has resisted the forces of sin and evil just as her father did.

Four months before Paul Carlson died he delivered a message in Lingala at the Wasolo Regional Church Conference. His message text was from 1 Peter 2:21-24:

"To this you were called, because Christ suffered for you, leaving you an example, that you should follow in his steps.... He himself bore our sins in his body on the tree, so that we might die to sins and live for righteousness; by his wounds you have been healed."

"At this conference," Paul began, "we are going to think about following Jesus. It is not hard to follow Jesus when all goes well, but sometimes it is difficult to follow Him when the road is difficult." After he described the state of persecution for Christ's sake in various regions in the Congo, he said, "We do not know what will happen in 1964, until we meet together again. We do not know if we will suffer or die during this year because we are Christians. But it does not matter! Our job is to follow Jesus." He went on to briefly describe, in simple New Testament logic the persecution experienced by the early church. "How does all of this apply to us at Wasolo?"

Paul asked. "Jesus is asking us if we are willing to suffer for Him. This is of the greatest importance to all of us Christians here today." Then Paul introduced the sacrament of Holy Communion. He said, "We are going to gather together at the Lord's Table. Before taking part, I think each person should ask themselves if they are willing to suffer for Jesus Christ if need be—and if he or she is willing even to die if necessary—during this coming year. Taking part in Communion means union with Jesus. Union with Jesus sometimes means joy—but union with Jesus sometimes means suffering. My friends, if today you are not willing to suffer for Jesus, do not partake of the elements. If you do take the cup and bread here today, be certain that you are willing to give your life for Jesus during 1964 or 1965 if it is necessary. To follow Jesus means to be willing to suffer for Him. Will you follow Jesus this year?"[117]

Within two months, many of the Congolese believers who heard this message and participated in Holy Communion suffered persecution unto death for Christ's sake. They, along with Paul Carlson, leave a testimony to us that inspires and challenges our faithfulness for Christ and His Kingdom.

* * * *

Jesus never dragged things out, never belabored a conclusion. He didn't wait until the end to bring it home. He was always bringing it home in ways that get our attention and make us think. He said what he wanted to say and ended. He left the listener to think about it and act accordingly. Jesus communicated with a style that said, "Here's the truth, now, you decide."

Eight simple lines, known as the beatitudes, help capture the essence of what it means to follow the crucified and risen Lord Jesus. Eight tracks of grace, founded in the Old Testament, fulfilled in the New Testament, and fundamental to the life of the Church, guide us in the Jesus way. The beatitudes are eight fundamental emotional attitudes, eight convictions of the soul, eight character qualities of the inner person. Jesus' soundtrack of the soul connects with our deepest longings, calms our fears, inspires our hope, and leads us along a path we never, ever, would have gone without him.

Notes

Chapter 1   Starting Over

1. William Barclay, *Beatitudes and the Lord's Prayer for Everyman* (New York: Harper Collins, 1975), 20.

2. *The New International Dictionary of New Testament Theology*, vol. 2, Colin Brown, ed. (Grand Rapids, Michigan: Zondervan, 1976), 824.

3. Charles W. Colson, *Born Again* (Old Tappan, New Jersey: Chosen Books, 1976), 109-113.

4. Colson, 112.

5. Colson, 113.

6. Colson, 114.

7. Colson, 117

8. Barclay, 24-25.

9. Barclay, 25.

10. Barclay, 25.

Chapter 2   Choosing Grief

11. Dallas Willard, *The Divine Conspiracy* (San Francisco: Harper, 1998), 116.

12. Barclay, 33.

13. Robert A. Guelich, *The Sermon on the Mount* (Waco, Texas: Word, 1982), 81.

14. Paul Watzlawick, *The Situation is Hopeless, But Not Serious* (New York: W. W. Norton & Company, 1993), 42-43.

15. Dallas Willard, *Renovation of the Heart* (Colorado Springs, Colorado: NavPress, 2002), 60.

16. John R. W. Stott, *Christian Counter-Culture: The Message of the Sermon on the Mount* (Downers Grove, Illinois: IVP, 1978), 40.

17. P. T. Forsyth, *God: The Holy Father* (Blackwood, South Australia: New Creation Publications, 1987), 13-14.

18. Forsyth, 14.

19. Barclay, 33.

Chapter 3   Understanding Power

20. Willard, *The Divine Conspiracy*, 117.

21. Eugene H. Peterson, "Growth: An Act of the Will," *Leadership* (Fall 1988), 40.

22. Augustine, *Sermon XXXI, Nicene and Post-Nicene Fathers, vol. 6,* ed. Philip Schaff (Peabody, Massachusetts: Hendrickson, 1995), 354.41

23. Helmut Thielicke, *The Evangelical Faith*, 3 vols. (Grand Rapids, Michigan: Eerdmans, 1977), vol. 2: 352.

24. Richard Longenecker, *The Christology of Early Jewish Christianity* (London: SCM, 1970), 74.

25. P. T. Forsyth, *God: The Holy Father*, 19.

26. Forsyth, 17.

27. Paul B. Long, *The Man in the Leather Hat* (Grand Rapids, Michigan: Baker Book House, 1986), 1-15.

Chapter 4   Feeding the Soul

28. P. T. Forsyth, *God: The Holy Father*, 14.

29. E. Stanley Jones, *The Christ of the Mount: A Working*

Philosophy of Life (London: Hodder and Stoughton, 1931), 29.

30. Peter Kreeft, *Back to Virtue* (San Francisco: Ignatius Press, 1992), 84-85.

31. John Stott, *Christian Counter-Culture*, 45.

32. John Chrysostom, *Homily XV, Nicene and Post-Nicene Fathers, vol. 10*, ed. Philip Schaff (Peabody, Massachusetts, 1995), 94.

33. Gerald F. Hawthorne, *Philippians: Word Biblical Commentary*, vol . 43 (Waco, Texas: Word Books, 1983), 166.

34. Kreeft, *Back to Virtue*, 156.

35. Kreeft, 157.

36. Kreeft, 154-155.

37. Eugene H. Peterson, "Should we pay more attention to the Lord's Day?" *Tough Questions Christians Ask*, ed. David Neff (Wheaton, Illinois: Victor Books, 1989), 13.

38. C. S. Lewis, *The Problem of Pain* (New York: Macmillan Publishing Co., 1973), 52-54.

Chapter 5   Showing Mercy

39. D. Martyn Lloyd-Jones, *Studies In The Sermon On The Mount*, 2 vols (Grand Rapids, Michigan: Eerdmans, 1971), vol. 1, 107.

40. Robert Guelich, *The Sermon on the Mount*, 105.

41. Dietrich Bonhoeffer, *The Cost of Discipleship* (New York: MacMillan, 1963), 124-125.

42. Eduard Schweizer, *The Good News According to Matthew*, trans. David E. Green (Atlanta: John Knox, 1975), 377.

43. Craig L. Blomberg, *Interpreting the Parables* (Downers Grove, Illinois: InterVarsity Press, 1990), 242.

44. Martyn Lloyd-Jones, *Studies in The Sermon on the Mount*, 101.

45. Richard B. Hays, *The Moral Vision of the New Testament* (San Francisco: HarperCollins, 1996), 103.

46. John Stott, *Christian Counter-Culture*, 149.

47. Helmut Thielicke, *The Waiting Father*, trans. John W. Doberstein (New York: Harper & Brothers, 1959), 163.

48. Martyn Lloyd-Jones, *Studies in The Sermon on the Mount*, 99.

Chapter 6   Purifying the Heart

49. Derek Kidner, *Psalms 1-72* (Downers Grove, Illinois, 1973), 114.

50. Dallas Willard, *The Divine Conspiracy*, 118.

51. John Stott, *The Christian Counter-Culture*, 49.

52. Søren Kierkegaard, *Purity of Heart Is To Will One Thing* (New York: Harper & Row, 1956), 178.

53. Kierkegaard, 48.

54. Kierkegaard, 57.

55. Kierkegaard, 108.

56. Kierkegaard, 107.

57. Kierkegaard, 108-110.

58. Kierkegaard, 110.

59. Kierkegaard, 54-55.

60. Kierkegaard, 61, 67.

61. Eugene H. Peterson, *Reversed Thunder: The Revelation of*

John and the Praying Imagination (San Francisco: Harper & Row, 1988), 60.

62. Kierkegaard, 70.

63. Kierkegaard, 72.

64. Michael Horton, "Seekers or Tourists?" *Modern Reformation* (July/August, 2001), 14.

65. Kierkegaard, 88.

66. Kierkegaard, 99.

67. Kierkegaard, 100.

68. Kierkegaard, 99.

69. Kierkegaard, 101.

70. Kierkegaard, 103.

71. Kierkegaard, 102.

72. Kierkegaard, 103.

73. Elizabeth Elliot, *Shadow of the Almighty: The Life and Testament of Jim Elliot* (New York: Harper & Row, 1958), 61.

74. Elizabeth Elliot, 88.

75. Elliot, 89.

76. Elliot, 196.

77. Elliot, 199.

78. Elliot, 212.

79. *Love Letters From Cell 92: The Correspondence Between Dietrich Bonhoeffer and Maria von Wedemeyer, 1943-45*, ed. Ruth-Alice von Bismarck and Ulrich Kabitz, trans. John Brownjohn (Nashville, Tennessee, 1995), 63-65.

80. M. Craig Barnes, *Sacred Thirst: Meeting God in the Desert of Our Longings* (Grand Rapids, Michigan: Zondervan, 2001), 84.

Chapter 7   Pursuing Peace

99. Martyn Lloyd-Jones, *Studies in The Sermon on the Mount*, 126.

Chapter 8   Suffering Persecution

100. Dietrich Bonhoeffer, *The Cost of Discipleship*, 100.

101. Paul Marshall, *Their Blood Cries Out* (Nashville, Tennessee: Thomas Nelson, 1997).

102. John Stott, *The Christian Counter-Culture*, 53.

103. Dietrich Bonhoeffer, *The Cost of Discipleship*, 127.

104. Duane Litfin, *Wheaton College Alumni Magazine* (Autumn, 2003), 64.

105. Vinay Samuel, "Religion: Cause or Cure for Terrorism? The Christian Church and a World of Religiously Inspired Violence," *SPU Response* (Seattle Pacific University magazine, Spring 2003), 10.

106. ITV News, "Abortion activist defiant in death," September 22, 2003 (www.itv.com/news/1763934.html).

107. John Perkins, *A Quiet Revolution* (Waco, Texas: Word Books, 1976), 190-191.

108. Dietrich Bonhoeffer, *The Cost of Discipleship*, 127.

109. Martyn Lloyd-Jones, *Studies in the Sermon on the Mount*, 132.

110. E. H. Robertson, *Christians Against Hitler* (London: SCM Press, 1962), 8.

111. Robertson, 18.

112. Robertson, 50-51.

113. Robertson, 32.

114. Tim Stafford, "The Joy of Suffering in Sri Lanka," *Christianity Today* (October, 2003), 57.

115. Mark Galli, "Now What? A Christian Response to Religious Terrorism," *Christianity Today* (October, 2001), 27.

116. John Howard Yoder, *The Politics of Jesus* (Grand Rapids, Michigan: Eerdmans, 1972), 112.

117. Lois Carlson, *Monganga Paul* (New York: Harper & Row, 1966), 127-130.

CPSIA information can be obtained
at www.ICGtesting.com
Printed in the USA
LVOW13s0259290617

539755LV00030B/960/P

9 781894 667913